Slave Narratives

Slave Narratives

THE GREENHAVEN PRESS COMPANION TO
Literary Movements and Genres

Slave Narratives

James Tackach, *Book Editor*

David L. Bender, *Publisher*

Bruno Leone, *Executive Editor*

Bonnie Szumski, *Editorial Director*

Stuart B. Miller, *Managing Editor*

David M. Haugen, *Series Editor*

Greenhaven Press, Inc., San Diego, CA

Every effort has been made to trace the owners of copy-righted material. The articles in this volume may have been edited for content, length, and/or reading level. The titles have been changed to enhance the editorial purpose. Those interested in locating the original source will find the complete citation on the first page of each article.

Library of Congress Cataloging-in-Publication Data

Slave narratives / James Tackach, book editor.
      p.   cm. — (Greenhaven Press companion to literary movements and genres)
    Includes bibliographical references and index.
    ISBN 0-7377-0550-7 (lib. bdg. : alk. paper) —
ISBN 0-7377-0549-3 (pbk. : alk. paper)
    1. American prose literature—Afro-American authors—History and criticism. 2. Slaves' writings, American—History and criticism. 3. Slaves' writings, American—Sources. 4. Slaves—United States—Biography—History and criticism. 5. Slavery in literature. 6. Afro-Americans in literature. 7. Autobiography—Afro-American authors. I. Tackach, James. II. Series.

PS366.A35 S57   2001
810.9'920625—dc21   APR - - 2001   00-037577
                                            CIP

Cover photo: Christie's Images/SuperStock
Dover, 105; Library of Congress, 43, 129, 160; National Archives, 75; North Wind Picture Archives, 95

CONTENTS

One literary source for the slave narrative was the Puritan captivity narrative of the seventeenth century. Both the captive and the slave are subjects of imprisonment, and both rely on the Christian God for deliverance from captivity.

Chapter 3: Expressions of Freedom in the Slave Narrative

Chapter 4: Gender Issues in the Slave Narrative

Chapter 5: The Slave Narrative's Enduring Legacy

narrative when crafting their fictional tales. Early African American novels such as William Wells Brown's *Clotel* and Frances E.W. Harper's *Iola Leroy* rely on slave narratives for their structure and subject matter.

In both theme and narrative strategy, twentieth-century African American autobiographies such as Richard Wright's *Black Boy* resemble the slave narratives of the previous century. Wright's story of his escape from the oppressively segregated South is indebted to slave narratives by Frederick Douglass and William Wells Brown.

Toni Morrison's *Beloved* has much in common with Harriet Jacobs's *Incidents in the Life of a Slave Girl*. Nonetheless, Morrison's novel differs from Jacobs's text in its emphasis on romantic love and the responsibilities of community rather than on the power of literacy.

FOREWORD

The study of literature most often involves focusing on an individual work and uncovering its themes, stylistic conventions, and historical relevance. It is also enlightening to examine multiple works by a single author, identifying similarities and differences among texts and tracing the author's development as an artist.

While the study of individual works and authors is instructive, however, examining groups of authors who shared certain cultural or historical experiences adds a further richness to the study of literature. By focusing on literary movements and genres, readers gain a greater appreciation of influence of historical events and social circumstances on the development of particular literary forms and themes. For example, in the early twentieth century, rapid technological and industrial advances, mass urban migration, World War I, and other events contributed to the emergence of a movement known as American modernism. The dramatic social changes, and the uncertainty they created, were reflected in an increased use of free verse in poetry, the stream-of-consciousness technique in fiction, and a general sense of historical discontinuity and crisis of faith in most of the literature of the era. By focusing on these commonalities, readers attain a more comprehensive picture of the complex interplay of social, economic, political, aesthetic, and philosophical forces and ideas that create the tenor of any era. In the nineteenth-century American romanticism movement, for example, authors shared many ideas concerning the preeminence of the self-reliant individual, the infusion of nature with spiritual significance, and the potential of persons to achieve transcendence via communion with nature. However, despite their commonalities, American romantics often differed significantly in their thematic and stylistic approaches. Walt Whitman celebrated the communal nature of America's open democratic society, while Ralph Waldo

Emerson expressed the need for individuals to pursue their own fulfillment regardless of their fellow citizens. Herman Melville wrote novels in a largely naturalistic style whereas Nathaniel Hawthorne's novels were gothic and allegorical.

Another valuable reason to investigate literary movements and genres lies in their potential to clarify the process of literary evolution. By examining groups of authors, literary trends across time become evident. The reader learns, for instance, how English romanticism was transformed as it crossed the Atlantic to America. The poetry of Lord Byron, William Wordsworth, and John Keats celebrated the restorative potential of rural scenes. The American romantics, writing later in the century, shared their English counterparts' faith in nature; but American authors were more likely to present an ambiguous view of nature as a source of liberation as well as the dwelling place of personal demons. The whale in Melville's *Moby-Dick* and the forests in Hawthorne's novels and stories bear little resemblance to the benign pastoral scenes in Wordsworth's lyric poems.

Each volume in Greenhaven Press's Companions to Literary Movements and Genres series begins with an introductory essay that places the topic in a historical and literary context. The essays that follow are carefully chosen and edited for ease of comprehension. These essays are arranged into clearly defined chapters that are outlined in a concise annotated table of contents. Finally, a thorough chronology maps out crucial literary milestones of the movement or genre as well as significant social and historical events. Readers will benefit from the structure and coherence that these features lend to material that is often challenging. With Greenhaven's Literary Movements and Genres in hand, readers will be better able to comprehend and appreciate the major literary works and their impact on society.

INTRODUCTION

The slave narrative is a uniquely American literary genre. As Henry Louis Gates Jr., a prolific scholar of African American literature, states:

> One of the most curious aspects of the African person's enslavement in the New World is that he and she *wrote* about the severe conditions of their bondage . . . . In the long history of human bondage, it was only the black slaves in the United States who . . . created a *genre* of literature that at once testified against their captors and bore witness to the urge of every black slave to be free and literate.[1]

Literary historians attest that between 1700 and the mid-twentieth century more than six thousand ex-slaves narrated their stories of bondage in books, pamphlets, and interviews. More than one hundred book-length slave narratives were published during that time period.

In the middle of the nineteenth century, particularly during the two decades before the Civil War, slave narratives were immensely popular with American readers. Frederick Douglass's first narrative, *Narrative of the Life of Frederick Douglass, an American Slave*, published in 1845, sold five thousand copies within four months of publication. Other slave narratives of that era enjoyed comparable sales figures. After the Civil War, interest in the stories of former slaves remained high. Booker T. Washington's *Up from Slavery*, published in 1901, became an immediate best-seller and was quickly translated into several European languages. During the next thirty years, millions of readers around the world purchased and read Washington's story.

Students of the twenty-first century might expect that scholarly interest in the slave narrative would have waned after 1865, when slavery was officially abolished by the Thirteenth Amendment to the U.S. Constitution, or at least by the latter decades of the twentieth century, when the last ex-slaves died. But the slave narrative as a genre is alive and well, thanks to the efforts of contemporary literary scholars and the interest of contemporary writers who still find in the slave narrative form a source for their own true and fictional stories.

Interest in the slave narrative did wane during the 1940s and 1950s, but the genre began to receive renewed attention during the 1960s, when the civil rights movement and black arts movement sparked a fresh interest in African American writing. During the final decades of the twentieth century, slave narratives long out of print, such as Harriet Jacobs's *Incidents in the Life of a Slave Girl*, were republished. Slave narratives were added to literary anthologies and high school and college course syllabi and were included in discussions at academic seminars and conferences.

Moreover, American writers, both white and African American, have long used the slave narrative to shape their own autobiographical and fictional stories. Notable American texts such as Harriet Beecher Stowe's *Uncle Tom's Cabin* (1852), Mark Twain's *Adventures of Huckleberry Finn* (1884), Richard Wright's *Black Boy* (1945), Ralph Ellison's *Invisible Man* (1952), Alex Haley's *Roots* (1976), and Toni Morrison's *Beloved* (1987) are, in either form or content, closely related to the slave narrative.

This anthology offers critical essays for students exploring the slave narrative. These essays discuss the genre's origins and development, its form and content, and its lasting impact on American literature. The collection aids the student investigating slave narratives in understanding and appreciating the original sources as well as exposes the student to the fresh insights of contemporary literary scholars who are examining with renewed vigor this uniquely American genre.

NOTE

1. Henry Louis Gates Jr., Introduction to *The Classic Slave Narratives*. New York: New American Library, 1987, p. ix.

THE SLAVE NARRATIVE:
AN AMERICAN GENRE

The first slaves came to America in 1619, but slaves' stories remained unrecorded for almost one hundred years. The tales of men and women in bondage were passed down orally from generation to generation, but not until the early eighteenth century did anyone commit to paper a slave's story. Between the beginning of the eighteenth century and the middle of the twentieth century, however, the life stories of several thousand slaves were recorded in a variety of media—books, pamphlets, broadsides, published interviews, newspapers, and magazines. The publication of these stories over a period of 250 years has resulted in the creation of a significant body of literary work, a major contribution to the American literary canon.

SOURCES

Although the American slave narrative is a uniquely American genre, American slave narratives, which first appeared at the beginning of the eighteenth century and reached maturity during the three decades before the Civil War, are rooted in a variety of literary forms and genres: African and African American folklore; the Bible; travel writing, particularly the journals of the first European explorers who surveyed the Americas; the Puritan spiritual autobiography; the picaresque novel; the domestic novel; the abolitionist press; the captivity narrative; and the American success narrative. Of those, the last two—the captivity narrative, as created by Mary Rowlandson, and the American success narrative, as formulated by Benjamin Franklin—are arguably the most profound influences on the form and content of the slave narrative. Like the slave narrative, both genres essentially developed on American soil.

Rowlandson's autobiographical story of a twelve-week captivity by Wampanoag Indians, published in 1682 as *The*

Narrative of the Captivity and Restoration of Mrs. Mary Row-landson, was one of the most widely read literary works of the American colonial period. In her narrative, Rowlandson describes her capture by the Wampanoags during King Philip's War (1675–1678), her life in captivity, her struggles to persevere during her ordeal, and her eventual release, for which she credits a benevolent and forgiving God. Many slave narratives fit Rowlandson's basic form. The slave narrator describes his or her capture in Africa (or his or her upbringing on a white man's plantation in America); his or her life in captivity, which often includes a frank description of slavery's most brutal aspects; and his or her eventual escape or release. Like Rowlandson's narrative, the slave narrative often credits the Christian God for giving the slave strength and perseverance to endure the most difficult moments of captivity and for allowing the slave to reach the promised land of freedom. For example, in *Narrative of the Life of Frederick Douglass, an American Slave*, published in 1845, Douglass details his life as a slave, describes the process by which he became a free man, and offers God "thanksgiving and praise" for giving him the "good spirit" to hold "a deep conviction that slavery would not always be able to hold me within its foul embrace."[1]

Franklin's *Autobiography* tells the story of a man who was born on the bottom rung of the American social order and rose to its very top. Through diligence and perseverance, Franklin, a candlemaker's son, became both wealthy and famous. At the opening of the *Autobiography*, Franklin asserts that he is writing so that his posterity might know of his journey from "the Poverty & Obscurity in which I was born & bred, to a State of Affluence & some Degree of Reputation in the World."[2] The American success narrative, as created by Franklin, became a model for the ex-slave who wished the public to know the story of his or her rise from slavery. Booker T. Washington's autobiography, *Up from Slavery*, published in 1901, is deeply indebted to Franklin's story of success. Washington's text traces his life from a plantation in Virginia to the presidency of Tuskegee Institute in Alabama.

THE FIRST SLAVE NARRATIVES

The first slave narratives were short and simple documents. Marion Wilson Starling and other literary historians identify

Adam Negro's Tryall, composed in 1703, as the first American slave narrative. Adam's narrative was actually a court document, the proceedings of two trials, during which Adam, a Massachusetts Bay Colony slave, tried to convince a judge and jury that his master had promised in writing, seven years before, to set him free in seven years. Adam told his story to the court, and a court record keeper recorded Adam's narrative. The narrative first appeared in the written transactions of the colonial Massachusetts court that heard his case.

Adam Negro's Tryall, like most slave narratives of the eighteenth century, was not actually written by the slave narrator. During the eighteenth century, the overwhelming majority of American slaves were illiterate; eventually many states would actually make it illegal to teach a slave to read and write—though some slave owners disobeyed the law, and some slaves, like Frederick Douglass, circumvented the laws and achieved literacy. And like Adam's narrative, most of the earliest slave narratives were quite short. For example, one early slave narrative, *The Life and Dying Speech of Arthur, a Negro Man,* the tale of a man executed for the crime of rape, was published in Boston in 1768 as a broadside, a single-page document.

OLAUDAH EQUIANO'S NARRATIVE

The first ex-slave to write his own story and publish it in book-length form was Olaudah Equiano, a native of Africa, born around 1745, kidnapped into slavery at age eleven, and freed in 1766. His narrative, *The Interesting Narrative of the Life of Olaudah Equiano, or Gustavus Vassa, the African,* published in London in 1789, became the prototype for scores of book-length slave narratives that would appear in the nineteenth century.

Equiano's narrative begins on the west coast of Africa, when the eleven-year-old Equiano is kidnapped, sold to white slave traders, and transported to America in a slave ship. The most riveting section of Equiano's narrative is the chapter devoted to a description of the journey to the New World. When the young Equiano is sent below the ship's deck, he reveals a nightmarish scene:

> The stench of the hold . . . was so intolerably loathsome, that it was dangerous to remain there for any time. . . . The closeness of the place, and the heat of the climate, added to the

number in the ship, being so crowded that each had scarcely room to turn himself, almost suffocated us. This produced copious perspiration, so that the air soon became unfit for respiration, from a variety of loathsome smells, and brought on a sickness among the slaves, of which many died. . . . This deplorable situation was again aggravated by the galling of the chains . . . and the filth of the necessary tubs, into which the children often fell, and were almost suffocated. The shrieks of the women, and the groans of the dying, rendered it a scene of horror almost inconceivable.[5]

Most slaves whose narratives were recorded were born on the American continent and could not supply information about the wretched sea voyage that brought African slaves to the New World. One of Equiano's most noteworthy contributions to the slave narrative genre is this vivid description of the journey to America, often called the Middle Passage. Historians inform us that about half of the slaves aboard the ships making the Middle Passage perished.

Equiano records his life as a slave, his exciting experiences as a deck hand aboard military ships during England's war with France, and his achievement of freedom (he purchased himself from his master with money he had managed to save during ten years of servitude). He also informs his readers of his life after slavery as a sailor and hairdresser. His narrative was published in London in 1789 and later in America.

FORM AND CONTENT

The book-length slave narratives that followed Equiano's carried, in the words of William L. Andrews, "a black message inside a white envelope."[4] These narratives, like Equiano's, opened with prefaces and introductions, written by white editors or supporters, that testified to the narrative's authenticity. These testimonials were necessary because the reading public was generally skeptical of the veracity of the slave's story. Many believed that slave narrators grossly exaggerated the hardships of slavery and fabricated their daring tales of escape. Thus, some editions of Equiano's narrative open with a preface, by an unnamed writer, that vouches for Equiano's reliability as a narrator: "Whenever he defended himself, FACTS were the foundation of his assertions; and no statement was made by him, for which he had not some voucher or authority."[5] Similarly, Frederick Douglass's 1845 narrative opens with two prefaces, composed by prominent white abolitionists William Lloyd Garrison and Wendell Phillips, that assert the accuracy of Douglass's story. Harriet Jacobs's *Incidents in the Life of a Slave Girl* contains an introduction by the white abolitionist writer Lydia Maria Child. The typical book-length slave narrative also contains appendices comprising freedom papers, letters of support, and other personal documents.

The narratives themselves often begin with the words "I was born," followed by the sketchy details of the slave's ancestry. Most narratives are chronologically organized, beginning with the slave's early childhood memories and concluding with the slave's achievement of freedom, often the result of a daredevil escape. Between birth and escape are chronicled the details of life under slavery—harsh living conditions, hard toil in the fields, and brutal punishments for neglect of duty. Despite these hardships, however, the slave narrator retains an optimistic spirit and a yearning for freedom; he or she simply refuses to be broken by the slave system. This desire for freedom eventually results in the slave's forming some plan to deceive his or her master and escape to the North, where slavery is prohibited by law.

Most of the book-length antebellum slave narratives were composed by men. The few authored by women provide a unique perspective into the institution of slavery. Mary Prince's *The History of Mary Prince*, published in 1831, and Harriet Jacobs's *Incidents in the Life of a Slave Girl*, published in 1861, both attest to the brutal sexual exploitation of female slaves. In addition, both narratives detail one of the most troubling aspects of American slavery—the division of slave families as a slave mother is sold in one direction and her children in another.

SLAVE NARRATIVES AND THE ABOLITIONIST MOVEMENT

As a genre, the slave narrative reached maturity during the three decades before the Civil War, when the American abolitionist movement gained momentum. Although American slavery had always had its critics—Samuel Sewall, the Puritan magistrate who penned the first American antislavery document; Benjamin Franklin; the Quakers—abolitionists were small in number before 1800. After the turn of the nineteenth century, however, the abolitionist ranks swelled and the antislavery movement shifted from the fringes to the mainstream of American political life.

In 1819 the American Congress engaged in a fierce debate that placed the issue of slavery on the front pages of the nation's newspapers. The territory of Missouri had requested admission to the Union as a slave state. At the time, the United States comprised eleven slave states and eleven free states. Admission of Missouri to the Union as a slave state would tilt the balance in the U.S. Senate in favor of the slave states. After fierce debate—a debate that galvanized America's disorganized abolitionist forces—Congress passed the Missouri Compromise, which allowed Missouri to enter the Union as a slave state and Maine to enter as a free state. That compromise temporarily defused tensions between the North and South, but the slavery issue suddenly came to the top of America's political agenda.

During the 1820s, a powerful religious revival, later known as the Second Great Awakening, swept America, and many of the clergymen associated with that movement preached against slavery on moral grounds. The abolitionist movement dovetailed other social movements that commenced during the 1820s and 1830s—prison reform, educational reform, the temperance movement, and women's rights. In 1829, David Walker, a free black man living in Boston, published *Walker's Appeal*, a treatise harshly condemning American slavery.

Some historians cite January 1, 1831, as the beginning of the American abolitionist movement. On that date, William Lloyd Garrison commenced publication of his antislavery newspaper, the *Liberator*. The first edition of the *Liberator* boldly asserted Garrison's purpose: "I shall strenuously contend for the immediate enfranchisement of our slave population. . . . I am in earnest—I will not equivocate—I will not excuse—I will not retreat a single inch—AND I WILL BE HEARD."[6] Garrison's paper spread the abolitionist message rapidly throughout the United States, and many Americans joined the antislavery crusade.

A few weeks after Garrison launched the *Liberator*, Mary Prince, a slave born in Bermuda, published her narrative, *The History of Mary Prince*, the first slave autobiography narrated by a woman. Like many earlier slave narratives, Prince's was written not by her—she was illiterate—but by a white man, Thomas Pringle, a British social reformer. Prince's narrative, which was published in London, originally comprised only twenty-three pages, but in that short document, Prince provided for her readers a view into the world of the female slave. Prince's narrative testified to the sexual exploitation of women held in bondage.

NAT TURNER'S REBELLION

During the summer of 1831, an event occurred in Virginia that intensified the tensions that were developing among Americans over the issue of slavery. In August a slave named Nat Turner, with sixty to eighty fellow slaves, staged a twelve-hour rebellion. Turner's comrades roamed the countryside, invading farmhouses and murdering their white inhabitants. By the time Turner's night of terror was complete, he and his followers had slain sixty people, including children. Turner's rebellion was quickly stifled, and Turner was eventually captured, then quickly tried and hanged for his offense. Before his death, however, from his jail cell, Turner narrated his story to a white attorney, Thomas Gray.

On November 25, two weeks after Turner's execution, Gray published *The Confessions of Nat Turner*, a pamphlet explaining Turner's cause and detailing with brutal honesty the murders that Turner and his lieutenants carried out in August. In his narrative, Turner defends himself as a messenger from God sent to smite the sinful slave holders. He claimed to have had visions of God and to have heard voices from the heavens encouraging him to commence his bloody work: "And on the 12th of May, 1828, I heard a loud noise in the heavens, and the Spirit instantly appeared to me and said the Serpent was loosened, and Christ had laid down the yoke he had borne for the sins of men, and that I should take it on and fight against the Serpent."[7] Turner's descriptions of his operation are vivid: "Miss Margaret, when I discovered her, had concealed herself in the corner, formed by the projection of the cellar cap from the house; on my approach she fled, but soon was overtaken, and after repeated fatal blows with a sword, I killed her by a blow on the head, with a fence rail."[8]

The Confessions of Nat Turner shocked the nation. Proslavery Americans—many of whom blamed Garrison's *Liberator* for inciting Turner's rebellion—saw Turner as Satan personified, temporarily delivered from hell to wage his bloody massacre. Abolitionists saw Turner's rebellion as a warning of things to come—a massive uprising of slaves that would violently purge slavery from the American continent. According to abolitionists, a more widespread slave revolt was inevitable unless the South peacefully abolished slavery.

THE GREAT SLAVE NARRATIVES

Literary historians consider Frederick Douglass's *Narrative of the Life of Frederick Douglass, an American Slave* and Harriet Jacobs's *Incidents in the Life of a Slave Girl* as the most important and influential slave narratives of the pre–Civil War period. Like all great American books, these two texts appeared at a critical moment in U.S. history; they carried the abolitionist message at precisely the time when Americans were undertaking a fierce debate over the slavery question. But Douglass's and Jacobs's narratives were not simply abolitionist treatises; they were skillfully written texts whose literary value has endured long after the issue of slavery was settled.

Douglass's *Narrative* appeared with the subtitle "Written by Himself." Though he received only a few formal lessons in reading and writing, by the time he escaped from slavery at about age twenty, Douglass had become highly literate. When he published his *Narrative* in 1845, he was working for William Lloyd Garrison's American Anti-Slavery Society as a spokesperson and lecturer. Even before his narrative appeared in print, Douglass was well known among abolitionists as an articulate and dynamic public speaker whose riveting story of his escape from bondage captivated audiences. The acquisition of literacy was for Douglass the "pathway from slavery to freedom."[9]

Like earlier slave narratives, Douglass's text vividly described the horrors of slavery. He had seen women flogged for disobeying their masters. He describes a slave fatally shot by a man merely because the slave had tried to avoid a whipping. Douglass testifies to the grinding toil and the inadequate food and clothing that were a part of the typical slave's life. Above all, Douglass's narrative bears witness to the dehumanization of life in bondage. He is never told his birthday. He is separated from his mother and siblings at a young age so that he never forms family bonds. When his master dies, he and his fellow slaves are gathered with the farm animals for a valuation of the master's estate. He is treated as a beast of burden, not a human being.

Nonetheless, throughout this ordeal, Douglass maintains the spirit that will eventually carry him to freedom. He becomes literate. He learns a useful trade—ship caulking. At a crucial moment, he physically fights back against a cruel overseer named Mr. Covey rather than submit to a beating. Douglass experiences dark moments when he sincerely wishes for an end to his miserable existence, but he refuses to surrender the hope of freedom. And by refusing to be broken by the slave system, Douglass asserts his humanity. "You have seen how a man was made a slave; you shall see how a slave was made a man,"[10] he boldly announces two-thirds of the way through his narrative. When Douglass finally achieves freedom, he dedicates himself to the abolitionist crusade; he becomes "engaged in pleading the cause of my brethren—with what success, and with what devotion, I leave those acquainted with my labors to decide."[11] Douglass's *Narrative* became a signal literary work in the abolitionist cause.

Between the publication of Douglass's *Narrative* in 1845 and Jacobs's *Incidents* in 1861, several important slave narratives came to print. *Narrative of William Wells Brown, a Fugitive Slave* appeared in 1847, and *Narrative of the Life and Adventures of Henry Bibb, an American Slave* was published two years later. Both adhered to the form set by Equiano and Douglass. Brown's and Bibb's narratives detailed their years of bondage and their escapes from slavery, and both narratives were packaged with written testimonies of authenticity by white supporters. Neither had the impact of Douglass's narrative, but both became valuable additions to the growing body of slave narratives used by abolitionists in their campaign.

Incidents in the Life of a Slave Girl appeared just before the outbreak of the Civil War. Harriet Jacobs used a pseudonym for her text; the narrative's byline reads Linda Brent, and that name is also used for the narrator throughout the text. Critic William L. Andrews speculates that Jacobs did not use her real name in her story because of her text's frank discussion of the complex sexual dynamics that marked her relationship with her male master, Dr. Flint. For example, when Flint threatens to rape her, Linda chooses to engage in a sexual relationship with another white man, Mr. Sands, with whom she eventually has two children. Linda is greatly troubled by the morality of her relationship with Sands, but she feels that an affair with him is the only way to ward off the predatory Flint.

Linda Brent does ultimately escape from Flint, but her escape is not the dramatic flight to the North typical of the male-authored slave narrative. Linda lacks the mobility of the male refugee slave; her escape is to the tiny attic of her grandmother's cabin, where she hides for several years, watching her children from afar as they pass by. Linda does finally flee to the North and settle in New York. While she is living there, a kind white employer purchases her freedom from the Flint family, which has inherited Linda after Flint's death. The narrative ends with Linda celebrating her permanent freedom from slavery.

When *Incidents in the Life of a Slave Girl* first appeared, some readers thought that the work was a novel because of its unusual and melodramatic plot twists. Many readers surmised that the book was authored by Lydia Maria Child, the abolitionist writer who wrote the introduction and edited the text. A reviewer of *Incidents*, writing shortly after the narrative was published, claimed to know its author and her story, but readers remained skeptical about the book's origins. The authorship of *Incidents* was not conclusively attributed to Harriet Jacobs until 1981, the result of research conducted by the scholar Jean Fagan Yellin.

POST–CIVIL WAR SLAVE NARRATIVES

Although the Civil War and the Thirteenth Amendment to the U.S. Constitution put an end to slavery on American soil, former slaves continued to publish their tales of bondage to a postbellum readership still eager to learn about the lives of slaves. The slave narratives published after the war, however, differed significantly from those written during the abolitionist period. Most of the pre–Civil War narratives were antislavery texts; they detailed the atrocities of the slave system and made passionate pleas for an end to slavery. For the former slave writing after emancipation, the slavery issue was already settled. These postbellum slave narratives did include chapters focusing on life on the plantation, but the texts devoted equal or more space to the accomplishments of the slave narrator after emancipation. For example, *The Life and Times of Frederick Douglass*, published in 1881 and revised in 1892, was several times the length of Douglass's original *Narrative*; the later text included material about Douglass's life during the Civil War and postwar years.

By far the most widely read post–Civil War slave narrative

was Booker T. Washington's *Up from Slavery*, published in 1901. Washington was born a slave on a Virginia plantation in 1856. He was nine years old when emancipation came. Thus, Washington deals with his life under slavery in only the first two chapters of a seventeen-chapter text, and he harbors none of the bitterness toward slavery characteristic of earlier slave narrators. Washington does welcome emancipation when it comes, but he asserts that African Americans who "went through the school of American slavery, are in a stronger and more hopeful condition, materially, intellectually, morally, and religiously, than is true of an equal number of black people in any other portion of the globe."[12]

Washington's aim in *Up from Slavery* is not to chronicle the evils of American slavery. His purpose is to record his impressive achievements after emancipation—his attainment of a solid education and his subsequent professional endeavors, which included teaching and, later, establishing Tuskegee Institute in Alabama and serving as its first president. Washington's narrative emphasizes the point that the freed American slaves can only truly escape from slavery when they have developed life and employment skills and secured a job to support their families. Like many post–Civil War slave narratives, *Up from Slavery* traces the narrator's attempt to enter the mainstream of American life.

THE WPA SLAVE NARRATIVES

One of the most impressive collections of slave narratives was compiled during the Great Depression under the auspices of the Federal Writers' Project, a program established within the Works Progress Administration (WPA), a federal agency designed to create public jobs for the unemployed. From 1936 through 1938, researchers working for the Federal Writers' Project interviewed more than two thousand former slaves and recorded their life stories in forty-one volumes. Many of these former slaves were still illiterate, and their stories would have died with them were it not for this ambitious federal oral history project.

The WPA slave narratives vary in length and substance. Most are several pages in length. Many slaves remembered slavery as a harsh and dehumanizing condition and spoke frankly to interviewers about slavery's most ruthless aspects. Hence, these narratives further validate the authenticity of the narratives by abolitionist slaves such as Douglass and Jacobs. Some of the WPA narratives, however, depict slavery as a benign institution, hardly different from the rigorous life on any mid-nineteenth-century farm. It is true that conditions for slaves varied from plantation to plantation. Some masters kept their slaves well fed and properly clothed and refused to separate slave families at the auction block. Many of the pre–Civil War slave narrators were refugee slaves who had escaped a life of hard toil and who were fierce critics of the institution of slavery; most contented slaves (with few exceptions) did not write their life stories. The WPA narratives provide a broad view of life under slavery, broader than the perception of slavery that one gets by reading one or two of the abolitionist slave narratives of the mid–nineteenth century.

Historians and literary critics who have examined the WPA narratives warn us, however, that not all are highly reliable. Most of the former slaves interviewed by the Federal Writers' Project were in their seventies or eighties, an age when memories might not be sharp or accurate. Moreover, many of those interviewed might be living in poor health and in poverty; hence, they might view the antebellum past with nostalgia. Historian Paul D. Escott offers another reason to question the reliability of the WPA narratives:

> The most formidable problem encountered in using the narratives is the problem of candor. The Civil Rights Movement was decades beyond the horizon in the 1930s when former slaves were interviewed, and southern blacks lived in the grip of a system of segregation that was nearly as oppressive as slavery. . . . They could not afford to alienate local white people or the agents of the federal government. . . . All the rules of racial etiquette had to be observed, and the informant had to give priority to appeasing his interviewer rather than telling the truth about the past. Thus some of the former slaves pulled their punches.[15]

Despite such problems, the WPA slave narratives constitute a rich body of first-person accounts of the lives of African Americans held in bondage.

The Slave Narrative's Enduring Legacy

By the 1970s, virtually all former slaves had died, but the form of the slave narrative remains alive. Writers of fiction and autobiography, both African American and white, since the middle of the nineteenth century have used the structure and content of the slave narrative in creative and original ways. The first published novels by African American writers—Frederick Douglass's *The Heroic Slave* (1853), William Wells Brown's *Clotel; or, The President's Daughter* (1853), Harriet Wilson's *Our Nig* (1859)—were slave narratives in fictional form. Harriet Beecher Stowe's *Uncle Tom's Cabin* (1852), the single most important piece of abolitionist writing, was also deeply indebted to the slave narrative form. In *The Key to Uncle Tom's Cabin*, published the year after the great novel appeared, Stowe, to defend her novel against critics who argued that it exaggerated the hardships of slavery, identified the sources that she consulted while writing *Uncle Tom's Cabin*. Stowe acknowledged that she used as a model for Uncle Tom the narrator of Josiah Henson's 1849 slave narrative, *Life of Josiah Henson*. Stowe also corresponded with Henry Bibb and Frederick Douglass while she wrote *Uncle Tom's Cabin*, and she appended *The Confessions of Nat Turner* to *The Key to Uncle Tom's Cabin*.

During the twentieth century, American writers continued to use the slave narrative as a model. Richard Wright's autobiography, *Black Boy* (1945), traces Wright's life in the segregated South and his eventual departure for Chicago during the 1920s. The text's form—the narrator's boyhood in an oppressive society and his escape to a freer environment in the North—mirrors the movement of many slave narratives. Ralph Ellison's influential novel *Invisible Man* (1952) takes a similar form. Ellison's unnamed narrator departs from a Tuskegee-like college in the South and migrates to New York, where he begins a life of political activism. In 1967 a white novelist, William Styron, published his novel *The Confessions of Nat Turner*, based on Turner's 1831 narrative. In 1971, Ernest Gaines published *The Autobiography of Miss Jane Pittman*, a novel about a one-hundred-year-old former slave who narrates her life story to a high school teacher as part of an oral history project.

Perhaps the most creative reworking of the slave narrative form in recent years is the novel *Beloved*, by Toni Morrison, the first African American to win the Nobel Prize in literature. Morrison's novel tells the story of Sethe, a slave woman who crosses the Ohio River to freedom in 1850 and later kills her infant daughter, Beloved, rather than allow her to be captured and returned to slavery. Throughout the novel, the ghost of Beloved haunts the home of Sethe and Denver, Beloved's surviving sister. Drawing on material from slave narratives, Morrison details the dehumanizing conditions of the slave system and, following in the tradition of Harriet Jacobs, illustrates the stresses that slavery placed on the African American family.

Why do American writers, literary scholars, and, apparently, readers continue to find the slave narrative so compelling? Perhaps because the slave narrative reminds Americans of their nation's most grievous sin, a blight on a country dedicated to the proposition that all are created equal. Or perhaps because America's history so closely resembles a slave's narrative. The nation began when thirteen British colonies escaped from captivity, set out on an unsteady course toward freedom, and once free produced significant achievements in the world. Perhaps American writers and readers keep returning to the slave narrative because it serves as both a history lesson and a parable of the American experience.

Recent evidence suggests that the slave narrative will continue to interest twenty-first-century American readers and scholars. In 1999, Yuval Taylor published a two-volume collection of slave narratives, each volume comprising ten unabridged narratives. Taylor's anthologies contain the most popular slave narratives, including those written by Douglass, Jacobs, and William Wells Brown. But Taylor's collection also includes narratives long out of print, such as those authored by J.W.C. Pennington and William Grimes. And on Martin Luther King Day in 2000, the actor James Earl Jones read excerpts from slave narratives by Douglass, Jacobs, Brown, Henry Bibb, Sojourner Truth, and others at a recitation in New York City. Evidence, indeed, that the slave narrative, like the slave narrator, will endure.

NOTES

1. Frederick Douglass, *Narrative of the Life of Frederick Douglass, an American Slave.* 1845. New York: Dover Publications, 1995, p. 19.

2. Louis P. Maser, ed., *The Autobiography of Benjamin Franklin.* Boston: Bedford Books, 1993, p. 27.

3. Olaudah Equiano, *The Life of Olaudah Equiano*, in Henry Louis Gates Jr., ed., *The Classic Slave Narratives.* New York: New American Library, 1987, p. 35.

4. William L. Andrews, Introduction to *The Civitas Anthology of African American Slave Narratives,* ed. Henry Louis Gates Jr. and William L. Andrews. Washington, DC: Civitas/Counter-

point, 1999, p. 6.

5. Equiano, *The Life of Olaudah Equiano*, p. 6.

6. Quoted in George M. Fredrickson, ed., *William Lloyd Garrison.* Englewood Cliffs, NJ: Prentice-Hall, 1968, p. 23.

7. Quoted in Kenneth S. Greenberg, ed., *The Confessions of Nat Turner and Related Documents.* Boston: Bedford Books, 1996, pp. 47–48.

8. Quoted in Greenberg, *The Confessions of Nat Turner,* p. 50.

9. Douglass, *Narrative,* p. 20.

10. Douglass, *Narrative,* p. 39.

11. Douglass, *Narrative,* p. 69.

12. Booker T. Washington, *Up from Slavery.* 1901. New York: Bantam Books, 1970, p. 11.

13. Paul D. Escott, *Slavery Remembered: A Record of Twentieth-Century Slave Narratives.* Chapel Hill: University of North Carolina Press, 1979, pp. 7–8.

CHAPTER 1

The Origins and Development of the Slave Narrative

Slave Narratives

The First Slave Narratives: Tales of Rogues and Runaways

Marion Wilson Starling

Marion Wilson Starling, a prominent scholar of
African American literature, is the author of *The
Slave Narrative: Its Place in American History* and
many essays on American slave narratives. In this
excerpt from *The Slave Narrative*, Starling discusses
the first three published slave narratives, by slaves
named Adam, Briton Hammon, and Arthur. These
early slave narratives, which were narrated by slaves
but recorded by literate whites, present outlaw protagonists who sought to escape from their lives under the institution of slavery. In many subsequent
slave narratives, the slave narrator would be an individual at odds with the white society that enslaves.

The first slave narrative was recorded in the transaction of
the Colonial Society of Massachusetts in Boston, County of
Suffolk, on August 3 and November 2, 1703, under the cap-
tion: *Adam Negro's Tryall.* Adam was the slave of one John
Saffin, a prosperous gentleman farmer of Suffolk County,
whose troubles with his slave we first learn of in the tract
which Saffin wrote and printed in Boston in 1701 in response to the recent publication by Samuel Sewall of the antislavery pamphlet, *The Selling of Joseph.*

ADAM'S TRIAL

It seems that Adam had not only capped a seven-year period
of work-dodging with flat refusal to accompany his master
when Saffin was obliged to leave town, but had taken advantage of Saffin's absence to terminate his indentureship,
going to Judge Sewall with a writ of promise Adam had ob-

Excerpted from Marion Wilson Starling, *The Slave Narrative: Its Place in American History, Second Edition.* Copyright © 1981, 1988 Marion Wilson Starling. Reprinted with permission from The Permissions Company, PO Box 243, High Bridge, NJ 08829, USA, on behalf of Howard University Press.

tained from Saffin seven years before to the effect that Saffin would give him his freedom after seven years of service. A few days after Saffin returned to Boston, Adam came to the house and informed him that he was to go see "Captain Sewall" at once. Saffin guessed instantly what Adam had been up to but determined not to let him have his freedom because he had in no way fulfilled the conditions of service. Saffin then went to see Sewall. The latter would not let him touch the paper which Adam had brought him but asked Saffin if he recognized the signature, which Saffin admitted was his own.

Sewall then tried to persuade Saffin to grant Adam his freedom, even though Adam might not have served Saffin as agreed upon. A Mr. Addington, who was with Sewall when Saffin arrived, advised Saffin against using the same standard in judging the behavior of Negroes as he would use on others, saying that there was "much to be allowed to the behaviour of Negroes, who are so ignorant, rude, and brutish, and therefore to be considered as Negroes." But Saffin would not give in, because, as he claimed, he had allowed Adam every kind of opportunity during the whole seven years to encourage him to be a good servant to him, and yet Adam had continually behaved "so diametrically contrary to those conditions" he simply would not agree to the manumission. Thereupon Adam provided himself with an attorney, one Thomas Newton, and the matter came to trial before the Court of General Sessions of the Peace for the County of Suffolk on August 3, 1703.

The evidence of the witnesses for John Saffin at the trial, including the various employers to whom Saffin had hired Adam out when he had finally decided that he himself could get nothing but headaches out of Adam, caused the jury to decide in favor of Saffin, ordering Adam's writ of manumission to be rescinded. Adam himself had not been able to refute their charges that he had been continually insolent and quarrelsome; that he would work when he wanted to—making a neat little profit for himself on a piece of "rich ground" which his master Shepard had given him to plant tobacco on for his own use—but would slyly make the others do the rest of the work; and that he would go off when he pleased and stay as long as he liked, returning so "proud and surlie" that no one dared to speak to him when he got back, lest he strike. Adam's reply was that he had not liked the way he had been ordered to do things by the different employers. For example, when one John Griffin of Castle Island had called him "Rascal" in the course of telling him to remove some earth, Adam had replied that he was "No Rascal, no Rogue, and no Thief," and had answered Clark's push with a push of his own, warning him that if he struck Adam, Adam would strike back. Clark then struck him with a stick, which Adam promptly broke, and "would have like to have spoilt him" with a shovel had not other laborers come to Clark's aid, carrying Adam off to a "dungeon."

Adam immediately appealed against the jury's decision that he was to remain Saffin's servant, and the appeal was heard at the next Court of Assize. In his appeal, Adam stressed the fact that there was no provision in Saffin's writ of promise whereby he was to forfeit his freedom if he did not serve his master or other employers assigned him by his master as well as they wanted him to. He said that Saffin had not made his promise of freedom subject to any conditions; besides, liberty was too great a privilege to be taken away from a man for anything so trivial or frivolous as the sauciness and laziness reported by Saffin. On November 2, 1703, at Her Majesty's Superiour Court of Judicature, Suffolk County, Judge Sewall presiding, the jury returned a verdict reversing the former judgment of the Court of General Sessions, with the concluding assertion:

> Its therefore Considered by the Court That the sd. Adam and his heirs be at peace and quiet and free with all their Chattles from the sd. John Saffin Esqr and his heirs for Ever.

BRITON HAMMON'S NARRATIVE

Though separated by nearly sixty years in time, the next slave narrative that we have shows a slave who resembles Adam in his flair for mapping out his own destiny without benefit of his master's sanction. A complete outline of the narrative appears in its incredibly long title:

> A Narrative of the Uncommon Sufferings, and Surprizing Deliverance of Briton Hammon, A Negro Man,—Servant to General Winslow, of Marshfield, in New-England; Who Returned to Boston, after Having Been Absent Almost Thirteen Years. Containing An Account of the many Hardships he underwent from the Time he left his Master's House, in the Year 1747, to the Time of his Return to Boston.—How he was cast away in the Capes of Florida;—the horrid Cruelty and inhuman Barbarity of the Indians in murdering the whole Ship's Crew;—

the Manner of his being carry'd by them into Captivity. Also, An Account of his being Confined Four Years and Seven Months in a close Dungeon;—And the remarkable Manner in which he met with his good old Master in London; who returned to New-England a Passenger, in the same Ship. (Boston; Printed and Sold by Green and Russell, in Queen-Street, 1760)

The narrative opens with a formal notice "To the Reader," in which Hammon apologizes for any deficiencies in the little book, on the ground that

> As my Capacities and Condition of Life are very low, it cannot be expected that I should make those Remarks on the Sufferings I have met with, or the kind Providence of a good GOD for my Preservation, as one in a higher Station; but shall leave that to the Reader as he goes along, and so I shall only relate Matters of Fact as they occur to my Kind.

SLAVE NARRATORS

In the introduction to his two-volume anthology of slave narratives, editor Yuval Taylor presents the characteristics of the typical slave narrator.

Whether before or after emancipation, the slave narrative, with very few exceptions, was written or dictated by a *former* slave. Especially before the end of the Civil War, these narrators by no means represented a cross section of the slave population. In the history of the institution in the United States, probably between 1 and 2 percent of the slave population managed to escape. The narrators thus tended to be unusually brave, physically strong, resourceful, and imaginative individuals. Most of them hailed from near the Mason-Dixon line. They were often literate; a large number had served as "house slaves" and had thus acquired some masters' knowledge of the world; most had excellent memories and superb analytic skills. In addition a disproportionate number of narrators were mulattos, who constituted only between 7 and 12 percent of the slave population—mulattos were not only more likely to be house slaves, but it was easier for them to pass as white when escaping. The narrators varied in age from their early twenties (Moses Roper) to their mid-seventies (James Mars). Between 10 and 12 percent of them were women (however, only one self-penned narrative of a female slave was published before 1865—Harriet Jacobs's 1861 *Incidents in the Life of a Slave Girl*).

Yuval Taylor, ed., Introduction to *I Was Born a Slave: An Anthology of Classic Slave Narratives.* Chicago: Lawrence Hill Books, 1999, p. xvi.

It seems likely that the pious note of this opening and the overwhelmingly pious closing page are interpolations of Hammon's scribe, as the body of the narrative is not at all in this tone. Hammon's adventures were self-sought, from the moment on that Christmas Day of 1747 when he decided to leave his master's house for a spree on the first ship he should find ready to set sail from the icy harbor at Plymouth. Teenage readers would enjoy his account of life among cannibalistic Indians off the coast of Florida, who fattened Hammon day by day on corn for the promise of a good big roast on their feast day; of his experiences in shipwrecks; of his long incarceration in a dungeon in Havana by pirates who could not induce him to board their ship; and of later adventures on gunboats. Life had sobered him up a trifle by 1760, so that he was prosaically engaged as ship's cook at the time of his romantic reunion with his master in London, which he describes rather winningly:

> I worked on board Captain Watt's ship almost three months, before she sail'd, and one Day being at work in the Hold, I overheard some Persons on board mention the name of Winslow, at the name of which I was very inquisitive, and having asked what Winslow they were talking about? They told me it was General Winslow; and that he was one of the Passengers. I ask'd them what General Winslow? For I never knew my good Master, by that Title before; but after enquiring more particularly I found it must be Master, and in a few Days Time the Truth was joyfully verify'd by a happy Sight of his Person, which so overcome me, that I could not speak to him for some Time—my good Master was exceeding glad to see me, telling me that I was like one arose from the Dead, for he thought I had been Dead a great many Years, having heard nothing of me for almost Thirteen Years.

ARTHUR'S NARRATIVE

Next in order of the slave narratives is *The Life and Dying Speech of Arthur, a Negro Man: Who Was Executed at Worcester, October 20th, 1768. For a Rape Committed on the Body of One Deborah Metcalfe* (Boston: Printed and Sold in Milk Street, 1768). The broadside on which Arthur's story is squeezed presents all the ingredients for a picaresque novel. Arthur himself was a character who would have delighted both a Smollett and a Dickens. He was born a slave in the house of one Richard Godfrey, of Taunton, Connecticut, in 1747, where he lived for fourteen years. He was taught to read and write and was treated kindly by his master. His mistress was so mean to him, however, that he ran away at the age of fourteen, setting out on a career of crime under the tutelage of a company of Indians at Sandwich. He relates:

> At Sandwich, I stole a Shirt, was detected, and settled the Affair, by paying twenty Shillings. My Character now being known, I thought proper to leave the Place; and accordingly shipped myself on board a Whaling Sloop, with Captain Coffin, of Nantucket: We were out eight months, and then returned to Nantucket, from whence we sailed, where I tarried six Weeks. In which Time I broke a Store of Mr. Roach's, from which I stole a Quantity of Rum, a pair of Trowsers, a Jacket, and some Calicoe.—The next Day I got drunk, and by wearing the Jacket, was detected, for which Offence I was whip'd fifteen Stripes, and committed to Gaol, for the payment of Cost, etc., from which I escaped in half an Hour, by breaking the Lock. Being now hardened in my Wickedness, I the next Night broke another Store in the same Place, from which I took several Articles, and then shipped myself on board a Vessel bound for Swanzey, where I was discovered, taken to Shoar, and whip'd sixteen [*sic*]; being then set at Liberty, I returned to Taunton, after one Year's absence, where my Master received me kindly, whom I served three Years: In which time I followed the Seas, sailing from Nantucket and Newport, to divers parts of the West-Indies, where I whored and drank to great excess. Being now weary of the Seas, on the 27th of October, 1764, I came again to live with my master at Taunton, where I behaved well for six weeks.

Having stood his vagaries longer than was to be expected, Arthur's master finally sold him to a Dutch gentleman, and after that sale Arthur changed owners frequently, without giving perceptible service to any. At length his crimes brought him the sentence which ended his life at the age of twenty-one. Far from being submerged by sadness at the thought of his approaching doom, Arthur enjoyed his rake's progress to the end. He tells of starting out on the last journey with a Mr. Jennison, who had the warrant for him:

> On our return to Rutland District, we stop'd at a Tavern in Hardwick, where after I had warmed myself, Jennison was Fool enough to bid me put along, and he would overtake me; accordingly I went out of the Door, and seeing his Horse stand handily, what should I do, but mount him, and rode off as fast as I could, leaving Jennison to pursue me on Foot. I got home before Bed-Time, and took up my Lodging in my Master's Barn for the Night, where I had a Bottle of Cherry-Rum (which I found in Mr. Jennison's Baggs) to refresh myself with.

> On the next day, being the 30th of March, 1767, was discovered, and committed to Worcestor Gaol, where I continued

'till the 20th of April following; at which Time I broke out with the late celebrated FRASIER, and a young Lad, who was confined for stealing. After which, at Worcester, we broke into a Barber's Shop, from whence we stole a Quantity of Flour, a Comb, and a Razor. We then set off for Boston. At Shrewsbury, we stole a Goose from Mr. Samuel Jennison, and from the Widow Kingsley in the same Place, we stole a Kettle, in which we boiled the Goose, in Westborough Woods. At Marlborough, we broke into a Distill-House, from whence we stole some Cyder Brandy. In the same Town we broke into a Shoe-maker's Shop, and took each of us a pair of Shoes. We likewise broke into Mr. Cip [*sic*] on Howe's House, in the same Place, from whence [*sic*] stole some Bread, Meat, and Rum. At Sudbury, we stole each of us a Shirt, and one pair of Stockings. At Weston, we stole some Butter from off a Horse. At Waltham we broke into a House belonging to one Mr. Fisk, from whom we took a small Sum of Money, some Chocolate and Rum. At Watertown we stole a Brass Kettle from one Mrs. White of that Place. My Companions now left me; upon which I went to Mrs. Fisk's in Waltham, who knew me: And having heard of my Escape from Worcester Gaol, immediately secured me, and with the Assistance of another Man, brought me back again, where on the 17th of September following, I was tryed and found guilty. Upon which, by the Advice of my Counsel, I prayed for the Benefit of the Clergy; which after a year's Consideration, the Court denied me: And accordingly I was, on the 24th of September last, sentenced to be hanged, which I must confess is but too just a reward for my many notorious Crimes.

Eighteenth-Century Narratives Offer a Mild Critique of Slavery

Frances Smith Foster

Frances Smith Foster, author of *Witnessing Slavery: The Development of Ante-bellum Slave Narratives* and other publications on slave narratives, discusses the characteristics of the slave narrative of the late-eighteenth century, when the slave narrative began to take shape as an identifiable literary genre. Although the protagonists of these late-eighteenth-century narratives "range from sinners to saints," according to Foster, they do not severely criticize the institution of slavery; the focus of these narratives is not slavery's most dehumanizing aspects. To illustrate her point, Foster uses *The Interesting Narrative of the Life of Olaudah Equiano, or Gustavus Vassa, the African*, the first widely distributed, book-length slave narrative, published in London in 1789.

Eighteenth-century slave narratives emphasized the individual, and for the most part they reflected the Puritan theocentric society. Race was a factor in the narrator's manner and matter, but it was not at first a crucial element. Their emphasis was upon a theme more easily identified with by all heirs to a Judeo-Christian philosophy, the struggle for existence as strangers in an inhospitable land.

One reason was that most of the eighteenth-century narratives were written and published in New England or London. In both places, slavery was not as commonplace as it was in the South and in the West Indies. Thus the early slave narrators were quite frequently introducing a subject which was only vaguely known to most readers. They found it more appropriate to present slavery as a philosophical issue and to emphasize problems such as the religious and moral contradictions of permanent bondage. Often discussion centered on the evils of the slave trade. Although no evidence exists of coteries comparable to those of the 1831–65 period, a few of the more popular narrators of the latter part of the eighteenth century knew and worked with each other on various antislavery projects. It is probable, therefore, that similarities in content and form during this time were not entirely coincidental.

The structural characteristics of the eighteenth-century slave narratives are traditional and simple. The narrative is a sustained chronological account of events in an individual's life presented to create or to prolong a particular response. Its purpose is to amuse its readers while encouraging them in their humanitarian and religious efforts. The account itself is preceded by introductory remarks that include confirmation of the narrator's good moral character and the validity of the narrative's facts by a respected white person. The narrative begins with accounts of the slave's life before captivity. This serves as exposition and as contrast with the later circumstances. The complication begins with the kidnapping of an innocent being and increases as the inconveniences and abuses of slavery become more evident. The narrative climaxes with rescue from slavery and a spiritual or material reward for the hardships encountered.

The depiction of the slave is more complicated. Generally, he is a primitive being who, while undergoing various hardships, nevertheless develops some of the traits which Westerners considered civilized and thus more human.

SINNERS AND SAINTS

The accounts of slaves in the eighteenth century present a series of characters who range from sinners to saints. But each of the narratives portrays an individual confronting a series of threatening incidents and having to rely quite extensively upon his courage and intelligence to survive. Sometimes this was manifest as rebellion or resistance, but at other times it was aggression. Many narrators sought out adventure as a way of achieving personal satisfaction. Olaudah Equiano, for example, encountered many of his problems because he would leave his master's sheep to buy and sell fruit, rum, and livestock for his personal gain. Richard Allen aroused the ire of persons because he refused to sit in the church balcony which was reserved for the black members. Instead, he led a group of blacks to build their own church. The protagonists of these narratives were not only reacting to situations, but they were also active participants in the situations.

Many of the narrators identified with the values of that society. This is not to say that they completely rejected the reality of their outsider status. Rather, it emphasizes the fact that their lives were not one continuous rejection of oppression and defense of manhood. Many of the early narrators display the contemporary attitudes and literary traditions of the times. Literature, they believed, could and should instruct and inform. Divine Providence controlled, but loyalty, thrift, and courage were essential.

The protagonist of the slave narratives at the end of the eighteenth century was a somewhat strange and exotic specimen, but one who was well educated or of high social status according to the standards of his primitive culture. This is evident in *Some Memoirs of the Life of Job* when the author [Bluett] states that Job could not only read and write but that "by his affable carriage, and the easy composure of his countenance, we could perceive he was no common slave." And it was true of other eighteenth-century narrators such as Olaudah Equiano, who was the son of a chief or "Embrenche," and Venture Smith, who was the son of a prince. The savage but noble concept that was so popular in eighteenth-century racial thought could explain the eighteenth-century narratives' predilection for highborn African narrators. It gives a basis for interpreting Bluett's reference to Job as "High Priest of Boonda" and the fact that so many titles of the eighteenth-century narratives heralded the narrator as being an African of noble birth.

The protagonist's experiences include traveling to various countries where he soon acquires a satisfactory amount of westernization. He then manages to receive his freedom, almost as a reward for good behavior. In fact, the slave has usually earned the respect and admiration of all who had recognized the resourcefulness and manly bearings of this diamond in the rough. Most often his experiences have included conversion to Christianity and the adoption of a Christian name. Ayuba Suleiman Diallo became Job; Olaudah Equiano was Gustavus Vassa; and Broteer Furro became Venture Smith. Thus there was a tendency to Anglicize the protagonist and to present the plight of the eighteenth-century African slave in terms very similar to those of the wandering hero legends or the religious Pilgrim's trials. Since he seems to have experienced little more physical pain or mental anguish than any other outsider in a new situation or any other lower-class individual in a class society, and he has in the process acquired or demonstrated characteristics usually associated with the Western hero, the "*African* gentleman," as Bluett calls Diallo, is little more than a variation upon traditional narrative archetypes.

In the eighteenth-century narratives, slavery is presented as a loss of physical freedom. Its dehumanizing aspects are not emphasized. Physical brutalities to slaves are presented as unusual occurrences and are usually remedied by sympathetic persons who intervene on the slave's behalf or by a polite discussion between master and slave. In Britain and its colonies, the evil of the system was still being weighed against the good. Thus discussions of the religious and moral contradictions within slavery were contained in the narratives, but the institution of slavery was not totally condemned. Rather, it was the abuses of the system by certain unscrupulous persons or by misunderstandings between slave and master which caused the exposure of conflicts within the system.

OLAUDAH EQUIANO'S NARRATIVE

A good example of the narratives written between 1760 and 1807 is *The Interesting Narrative of the Life of Olaudah Equiano, or Gustavus Vassa, the African,* first published in 1789. Equiano's narrative begins with an account of the geography and culture of his native country, Benin (part of the present-day Nigeria). He details family history, his childhood, his kidnapping, his enslavement and subsequent experiences in England, the West Indies, and the American colonies of Virginia and Georgia. Among his achievements he lists playing the French horn, reading the Bible, and hairdressing. During his varied experiences as a slave, he also learns the techniques of desalinization, navigation, and naval warfare. As a convert to Christianity, he debates with learned British Protestant ministers as well as Portuguese Catholic clergy. He eventually travels to every major area of the world, including the North Pole. After numerous misfortunes and many instances of salvation by God's direct intervention or his own quick thinking, he earns his freedom, claims England as his home, and works actively in anti-slavery activities.

Equiano's narrative is in many ways typical of those that were published between 1760 and 1807. The narrator is a person of more than usual independence, daring, and curiosity. In the tradition of much of eighteenth-century popular literature, the focus of the narrative is upon the individual and his adventures. Slaves such as Equiano were more like Defoe's Robinson Crusoe than Defoe's characterization of the ever-faithful and servile black man, Friday. For these daring men, capture by hostile Indians, shipwrecks on deserted islands, and military combat on the high seas were occasions to demonstrate their courage and intelligence. In addition, they were usually interpreted as manifestations of God's power and grace. They reinforce the Christian idea that for those who keep the faith, good does eventually come from evil. More often than not, the slave hero not only benefits himself but also positively influences the lives of his white masters and fellow workers. Thus he earns the respect and admiration of all men of good repute and noble character, while exemplifying God's salvation, which extends to all mankind.

Olaudah Equiano relates an experience which occurred during a voyage from the West Indies to Georgia that shows both of these themes. "On the fourth of February, which was soon after we had got into our new course," says Equiano, "I dreamt the ship was wrecked amidst the surfs and rocks, and that I was the means of saving everyone on board." He had this same dream three nights in a row. Soon after this, while on watch, he actually saw the rocks. The captain did not listen to his warnings, and the ship was wrecked. Equiano states:

> And in the midst of my distress, while the dreadful surfs were dashing with unremitting fury among the rocks, I remembered the Lord, though fearful that I was undeserving of forgiveness, and I thought that as he had often delivered he might yet deliver; and, calling to mind the many mercies he had shown me in times past, they gave me some small hope that he might still help me. I then began to think how we might be saved; and I believe no mind was ever like mine so replete with inventions, and confused with schemes, though how to escape death I knew not.

Equiano took over the management of the ship; for as he reports the captain was incapable of directing any escape attempt and most of the sailors gave up hope and proceeded to get drunk. Equiano declares:

> There were only four people that would work with me at the oars, and they consisted of three black men and a Dutch Creole sailor; and, though we went with the boat five times that day, we had no others to assist us. But, had we not worked in this matter, I really believe the people could not have been saved; for not one of the white men did anything to preserve their lives; indeed, they soon got so drunk that they were not able, but lay about the deck like swine, so that we were at last obliged to lift them into the boat, and carry them on shore by force. This want of assistance made our labor intolerably severe; insomuch, that, by going on shore so often that day, the skin was partly stript off my hands.

THE

INTERESTING NARRATIVE

OF

THE LIFE

OF

OLAUDAH EQUIANO,

OR

GUSTAVUS VASSA,

THE AFRICAN.

WRITTEN BY HIMSELF.

Behold, God is my salvation ; I will trust, and not be afraid, for the Lord Jehovah is my strength and my song ; he also is become my salvation. And in that day shall ye say, Praise the Lord, call upon his name, declare his doings among the people. Isa. xii. 2. 4.

EIGHTH EDITION ENLARGED.

NORWICH:

PRINTED FOR, AND SOLD BY THE AUTHOR.

1794.

PRICE FOUR SHILLINGS.

Formerly sold for 7s.

[*Entered at Stationers' Hall.*]

The title page of Olaudah Equiano's narrative

When all were safely on the island, he says, "I could not help thinking, that if any of these people had been lost, God would charge me with their lives; which, perhaps, was one cause of my laboring so hard for their preservation."

Besides a basically episodic structure, the narratives share a peculiar impersonal tone. While the hero's physical situation is greatly affected by the outcome of these occurrences, and while his moods may vary from despair to exaltation in the narration of events, his basic psychological well-being (that is, his concept of who he is and what his relationship to society ought to be) is not seriously questioned. Often the reader is amused, intrigued, sometimes astonished by the resiliency and resourcefulness of the individual. The reader is not pulled into a journey of tears and sighs, nor is he continuously terrified by the harsh and foreboding situations that challenge and threaten the narrator. His faith in God is almost identical to that which the narrator professes, for, inevitably, the slave is a Christian convert. Consequently, the ultimate result is known, and the interest is in the ways God's will is made manifest.

The intent of many eighteenth-century narratives to justify the ways of God to man is made very clear in the preface to James Albert Ukawsaw Gronnioaw's narrative:

> His long and perilous journey to the coast of Guinea, where
> he was sold for a slave, and so brought into a Christian land;
> shall we consider this as the alone effect of a curious and in-
> quisitive disposition? Shall we, in accounting for it refer to
> nothing higher than the mere chance & accidental circum-
> stances? Whatever Infidels & Deists may think, I trust the
> Christian reader will easily discern an all wise and omnipo-
> tent appointment in the direction of these movements. . . .
> God has put singular honor upon him in the exercise of his
> faith and patience, which, in the most distressing and pitiable
> trials and calamities have been found to the praise and glory
> of God.

Equiano is predisposed to the same justification: "I had a
mind in which every thing uncommon made its full impres-
sion, and every event which I considered as marvellous.
Every extraordinary escape, or signal deliverance, either of
myself or others I looked upon to be effected by the interpo-
sition of Providence."

Another purpose was to remind the Christian reader of
the sins of mankind. In the preface to *A Narrative of the Life
and Adventures of Venture, a Native of Africa,* the reader is
reminded that Venture's sufferings occurred in a Christian
country. "And," continues the preface, "if he [the reader]
shall derive no other advantage from perusing the narrative,
he may experience those sensations of shame and indigna-
tion that will prove him to be not wholly destitute of every
noble and generous feeling."

These religious functions were not intended to neutralize
the antislavery thrust, however. The narratives clearly show
that there were significant differences in the experiences of
these black writers and those of other writers. Unlike the Indian captives or prisoners of war, these narrators were
legally chattel for life. Physical freedom was not assured after a given time of servitude or after escape from one's captors. Equiano makes it clear that even those blacks who
were free could not anticipate the same respect and protection as whites. He tells the story of Joseph Clipson, who was
kidnapped from a vessel, "although he showed a certificate
of his being born free in St. Kitt's, and most people on board
knew that he served his time to boat building, and always
passed for a free man." Equiano adds:

> I have since often seen in Jamaica and other islands, free
> men, whom I have known in America, thus villainously

trepanned and held in bondage. I have heard of two similar practices even in Philadelphia: and were it not for the benevolence of the quakers in that city, many of the sable race, who now breathe the air of liberty, would, I believe, be groaning indeed under some planter's chains.

It is obvious in eighteenth-century slave narratives that many of the misfortunes suffered by the narrator were caused by nothing more than the condition of being black and a slave or of being black and yet not totally free. Equiano provides one of the many examples of the precariousness of the black narrators' existence:

> One Sunday night, as I was with some negroes in their master's yard, in the town of Savannah, it happened that their master, one Doctor Perkins, who was a very severe and cruel man, came in drunk; and not liking to see any strange negroes in his yard, he and a ruffian of a white man, he had in his service, beset me in an instant, and both of them struck me with the first weapons they could get hold of. I cried out as long as I could for help and mercy; but, though I gave a good account of myself, and he knew my captain, who lodged hard by him, it was to no purpose.

Equiano relates that he was left for dead. The next morning he was picked up and placed in jail. After a search, his master found him. Equiano states, "My captain on this went to all the lawyers in the town for their advice, but they told him they could do nothing for me as I was a negro."

Even when slavery is not the direct cause of the incident, the institution of slavery permeates the narratives. The environment in which the narrator lives, the resources available to him during his crises, the humor or bitterness with which the tale is told—all are connected to the conditions of bondage and freedom and are an important part of the story.

In the narratives of the eighteenth century, there was opposition to slavery on moral, religious, economic, and social grounds, but the prime object of attack during the eighteenth century was the slave trade and not the owners of slaves or the institution itself. As the debate continued, it was generally felt that if the slave trade were abolished, the system would not survive or at least would find it necessary to institute more humanitarian procedures. Thus when the African Slave Trade Act, which prohibited the importation of slaves into the United States, was signed by Thomas Jefferson in 1807, the general public felt slavery had received its deathblow. Interest in the narratives declined and the first period was ended.

Nineteenth-Century Narratives Condemn a Dehumanizing System

William L. Andrews

William L. Andrews, a prominent scholar of African American literature, has edited several collections of slave narratives, including *The Civitas Anthology of African American Slave Narratives* and *Black Women's Slave Narratives*. He has also written several important essays on this subject. In this essay, Andrews identifies the key features of slave narratives of the mid-nineteenth century. These narratives, according to Andrews, present a severe critique of the institution of slavery. The protagonists of many of these narratives, once free, become activists in the abolitionist cause. This excerpt from the introduction of *The Civitas Anthology of African American Slave Narratives* focuses on three of the most influential slave narratives of this period—those authored by Mary Prince, Nat Turner, and Frederick Douglass.

The great nineteenth-century slave narratives typically carry a black message inside a white envelope. Prefatory (and sometimes appended) matter by whites, such as [William Lloyd] Garrison's preface to [Frederick] Douglass's *Narrative* or Amy Post's letter of recommendation appending [Harriet] Jacobs's *Incidents in the Life of a Slave Girl,* attests to the reliability and good character of the narrator. Sometimes these "authenticating documents" shed light on the conditions under which the narrative was composed and written. The texts that set the tone for the classic slave narratives of the 1830–1865 era—*The History of Mary Prince* (1831) and *The Confessions of Nat Turner* (1831)—begin with detailed commentary on the circumstances of composition as well as the character and bearing of the slave himself or herself. Thomas R. Gray, the Virginia lawyer who interviewed Turner before his execution for his part in the greatest slave revolt in U.S. history, reports: "By permission of the Jailor, I have had ready access to [Turner], and finding that he was willing to make a full and free confession of the origin, progress and consummation of the insurrectory movements of the slaves of which he was the contriver and head; I determined for the gratification of public curiosity to commit his statements to writing, and publish them, with little or no variation, from his own words. That this is a faithful record of his confessions, the annexed certificate of the County Court of Southampton, will attest." Thomas Pringle, the British reformer who financed the publication of *The History of Mary Prince,* explains in his preface: "The narrative was taken down from Mary's own lips by a lady who happened to be at the time residing in my family as a visitor. It was written out fully, with all the narrator's repetitions and prolixities, and afterwards pruned into its present shape; retaining, as far as was practicable, Mary's exact expressions and peculiar phraseology. No fact of importance has been omitted, and not a single circumstance or sentiment has been added."

A Rite of Passage

Moving past the white-authored prefaces and recommendation letters to the actual narrative supplied by the fugitive slave, we find a story that centers on a rite of passage from slavery (usually in the South) to freedom (usually in the North, though sometimes the quest does not end until the fugitive's arrival in Canada or Great Britain). Usually the antebellum slave narrator portrays slavery as a condition of extreme physical, intellectual, emotional, and spiritual deprivation, a kind of hell on earth. Precipitating the narrator's decision to escape is some sort of personal crisis, such as the sale of a loved one or a dark night of the soul in which hope contends with despair for the spirit of the slave. Impelled by faith in God and a commitment to liberty and human dignity comparable, the North American slave narrator often stresses, to that of the Founding Fathers of the United States, the slave undertakes an arduous quest for freedom that climaxes in his or her arrival in the North. In many antebellum narratives, the attainment of freedom is signaled not simply by reaching the free states but by renaming oneself and dedicating one's future to antislavery activism. Douglass and Brown provide particularly memorable accounts of the act of self-naming and their discovery of a profession in antislavery activism, lecturing, and writing.

To ensure the absolute factuality of slave narratives and to rebut charges from defenders of slavery that the narratives were distorted by biased abolitionist editors and ghostwriters, the antislavery movement in the mid-1840s made a priority of publishing narratives by slaves who could write their own stories. Although Frederick Douglass was by no means the first fugitive slave to write his own narrative, his was among the first to feature the subtitle *Written by Himself* on the title page of his *Narrative*. One of the reasons why Douglass's *Narrative* became the epitome of the slave narrative in the antebellum era was its powerful evocation of the idea of literacy as the key to individual dignity, freedom, and opportunity. After Douglass's *Narrative*, the presence of the subtitle *Written by Himself* on slave narratives such as [William W.] Brown's and [Henry] Bibb's, and *Written by Herself* in the case of Jacobs's, testified to the African American author's dedication to literary self-determination. Thus the quest for physical freedom became intertwined in the work of a Douglass or Jacobs with the emergence from ignorance and unself-consciousness to knowledge and a sense of mission and social purpose.

MARY PRINCE'S UGLY BUT NECESSARY TRUTH

One reason for identifying Mary Prince as a harbinger of the classic American slave narrator is her narrative's eloquent testimony to the tenacious integrity of her own selfhood despite overwhelming efforts to subvert it and brutalize her. The extensive detailing of atrocities suffered by Prince from her earliest childhood, on which so much of the *History* focuses, reminds us that this narrative was published by an English antislavery society and undoubtedly was intended to serve the society's propaganda interests. As her sponsor and editor, Thomas Pringle, comments in his preface, personal statements like Prince's guaranteed that "good people in England might hear from a slave what a slave had felt and suffered," instead of depending solely on what antislavery agitators thought about slavery and the slave. But more remarkable in Prince's *History* than her patience with and endurance of the wrongs done to her by a succession of West

Indian masters is her gradual resistance, both verbal and physical, to her oppressors. The *History* shows how Prince refused the role of victim, choosing instead a series of strategies that would enable her to gain her freedom.

As important as Prince's example is in inaugurating black women's autobiography in the Americas, her active pursuit of freedom and the opportunity to voice her protest against slavery through the publication of her story underline the importance of this text to the evolution of the slave narrative tradition. Readers should note the fact that Prince approached her editor, Thomas Pringle, with the specific suggestion of writing her history. Hers was among the earliest slave narratives designed to tell the ugly but necessary truth about a socioeconomic system in the British West Indies that few people in England understood apart from the propaganda of the slaveowners. The way Prince tells that truth, both in the detail with which she recounts atrocities and in the frankness with which she speaks of many West Indian whites, must have surprised, if not shocked, many of her readers. Women, particularly those of Prince's caste and class, were not expected to speak out so bluntly in public, especially about their supposed betters. According to the prevailing standards of "true womanhood" in the early nineteenth century, a white woman would risk the charge of "unsexing" herself, of deserting her proper station in life and becoming something unnatural and morally perverse, by speaking out publicly against well-placed and presumably respectable men and women. A black woman who assailed her supposed betters risked even worse reprisals from whites. The racist mythology of the era did not treat black women as women but as breeding animals who had no right to even the limited degree of self-regard that white women were allowed in a male-dominated culture.

Mary Prince argues implicitly against this mythology by showing how cruel whites pushed her to the limits of her endurance. Only by talking back, saying no, and finally refusing to live any longer with her last master and mistress, the abusive Mr. and Mrs. John Woods, could Prince hope to preserve her physical and mental health and someday return to her husband. Her story concludes with a notable assertion from a black woman: "I know what slaves feel—I can tell by myself what other slaves feel, and by what they have told me. The man that says slaves be quite happy in slavery—that they don't want to be free—that man is either ignorant or a lying person." In this remark a black female slave declares herself to be a more reliable authority on slavery than any white man and to be fully capable of speaking for all her fellow slaves, both male and female, against any white man. The implication of this declaration should not be underestimated, since it constitutes the first claim in the African American autobiographical tradition for the black woman's authority as a spokesperson for *all* black people, regardless of sex, on the subject of "what slaves feel" about the morality of slavery.

NAT TURNER'S INSURRECTION

The Confessions of Nat Turner was the first North American slave narrative to receive wide attention in the United States and particularly in the South. Unlike later classic slave narratives of the antislavery crusade, however, Turner's *Confessions* was not written by someone sympathetic to the slave in question or to the cause of emancipation in general. Turner's amanuensis, Thomas R. Gray, was a Virginia lawyer and one-time slaveowner who published the *Confessions* partly to enrich himself and partly to quell the rumors of impending servile insurrection that had whipsawed the South since Turner's actual uprising. In the first sentence of the *Confessions*, Gray announces, "The late insurrection in Southampton has greatly excited the public mind, and led to a thousand idle, exaggerated and mischievous reports," which he intends to dispel by enabling whites "to understand the origin and progress of this dreadful conspiracy, and the motives which influence its diabolical actors." By naming Turner's action an "insurrection" and a "conspiracy," Gray aims from the start to prejudice his readers as to who Turner was and how he should be understood. As an insurrectionist, Turner was by definition the leader of an unwarranted revolt against civil authority and the constituted government of the land.

Yet the first time the condemned slave gets a chance to speak in the *Confessions*, in the opening statement of what is purportedly Turner's oral narrative, we read: "SIR,—You have asked me to give a history of the motives which induced me to undertake the late insurrection, *as you call it*" (emphasis added). Replying to Gray in this way sets the tone for the entire narrative, in which Turner and Gray vie for the power to define Turner. Gray has the first and last word, we might say, because he writes the prefatory and concluding documents, leaving Turner with the narrative middle, which is not, of course, a text one can regard without some skepticism since Gray wrote this part of the text too. Still in reading Turner's narrative it is important to recognize the ways in which the condemned man attempted to represent himself according to his own lights, so that his sense of self and his understanding of his mission and its justification would not be buried under the weight of Gray's hostile rhetoric. . . .

The Confessions of Nat Turner plainly challenged this image of the Negro as a constant, lacking the motive or potential for change unless and until factored into the white man's equation. We should not overlook the important fact that the *Confessions* contains the first significant chronology of an African American life in the literature of the American South. The simple but unprecedented import of the "confession" Turner recounts lies in his making a history of *himself,* when all Gray asked him for was "a history of the motives" that led to his uprising. From the outset of his portion of the *Confessions,* Turner announces that to give a proper accounting of his motives, "I must go back to the days of my infancy, and even before I was born." Turner then makes a crucial statement that interjects him irreversibly into history: "I was thirty-one years of age the 2nd of October last, and born the property of Benj. Turner, of this county." What follows is Turner's personal story, carried through a discernible beginning, middle, and end, and bearing an authority and conviction that left Gray both appalled and fascinated: "The calm, deliberate composure with which he spoke of his late deeds and intentions, the expression of his fiend-like face when excited by enthusiasm, still bearing the stains of the blood of helpless innocence about him; clothed with rags and covered with chains; yet daring to raise his manacled hands to heaven, with a spirit soaring above the attributes of man; I looked on him and my blood curdled in my veins." In the end, Gray tries to explain Turner away with labels such as "fanatic," "madman," and "fiend." But Turner remains elusive; something about him is masked and unfathomable. "He is a complete fanatic, or plays his part most admirably," Gray admits. Thus we are left to wonder, even as Gray seems to have wondered, if Turner's *Confessions* is really a confession at all. Gray hoped he was recording the confession of a crime. But many readers today think it sounds more like a confession of faith, the faith of a man convinced that he was about to be martyred for having led a divinely sanctioned holy war. These tensions within the text are one of the main reasons why Turner and his *Confessions* remain so provocative in the American national imagination as well as in the slave narrative tradition.

FREDERICK DOUGLASS'S MENTAL AND PHYSICAL FREEDOM

Frederick Douglass, author of the most influential African American text of his era, rose through the ranks of the anti-slavery movement in the 1840s and 1850s to become the most electrifying speaker and commanding writer produced by black America in the nineteenth century. With the publi-cation in 1845 of the *Narrative of the Life of Frederick Douglass, an American Slave, Written by Himself,* the antebellum slave narrative reached its epitome. Among slave narratives only Turner's *Confessions* challenged Douglass's *Narrative* for best-seller status in nineteenth-century America. In his own time Douglass's readership far outstripped that of such well-known white autobiographical writers as Henry David Thoreau, Margaret Fuller, and Walt Whitman. Douglass's writing, which eventually comprised three autobiographies, a short novel, and a substantial amount of journalism and oratory, was devoted primarily to the creation of a heroic image of himself designed to elevate the image of the slave in white Americans' eyes, to demonstrate the full potential of black people for freedom and a productive life as American citizens, and to inspire in African Americans the belief that color need not be a permanent bar to their achievement of the American Dream.

William Lloyd Garrison, Douglass's abolitionist mentor, introduced his *Narrative* by stressing how representative Douglass's experience of slavery had been. But Garrison could not help but note the extraordinary individuality of this black author's manner of rendering that experience. It is Douglass's style of self-presentation, through which he recreated the slave as an evolving self bound for mental as well as physical freedom, that has made his autobiography so memorable. In Douglass's *Narrative* the interlocking themes of freedom and literacy are given classic expression in African American literature. In the narratives of less gifted fugitive slaves, freedom is portrayed as a physical place—the

North, or Canada or Great Britain—or, most pragmatically, as an economic condition, in which the African American can finally achieve self-sufficiency and dignity through independent work. Douglass's *Narrative* adds to these notions of freedom a more idealized dimension—freedom is a state of mind and spirit characterized by unrestrained self-expression through language, both spoken and written. This is why Douglass's *Narrative* does not conclude with his successful flight to the North but with his first foray onto the antislavery lecture platform several years thereafter. To Douglass the power to use language to change the minds of others is the greatest power that an individual can exert and the most compelling sign of that individual's freedom. Ultimate freedom inheres in the power of self-expression—to speak freely what is on one's mind and in one's heart. Douglass's *Narrative* testifies to this freedom both in its climactic portrayal of its protagonist freely speaking out against slavery and in the demonstrated fact of Douglass's having become a writer who authors his own story and thus participates in the great tradition of American literary individualism through autobiography.

In the history of African American literature, Douglass's importance and influence are virtually immeasurable. His *Narrative* gave the English-speaking world the most compelling and sophisticated rendition of an African American selfhood ever fashioned by a black writer up to that time. Douglass's literary artistry invested this model of selfhood with a moral and political authority that all aspirants to the role of African American culture hero—from Booker T. Washington to Malcolm X—have had to come to terms with in their own autobiographies and in their public careers.

The Postbellum Slave Narrative: Assuming the Responsibilities of Freedom

Frances Smith Foster

In this excerpt from her book *Written by Herself: Literary Production by African American Women, 1746–1892*, Frances Smith Foster discusses some of the differences between the antebellum slave narrative and the slave narratives published after the Civil War. Using Elizabeth Keckley's *Behind the Scenes* as a model, Foster identifies some of these differences. The postbellum slave narrative focused on the ex-slave's achievements after emancipation rather than on the hardships endured during slavery. The postbellum narrative also featured a narrator who presented herself as a strong resistor against oppression rather than as a meek victim of it.

Unlike [Harriet] Jacobs, . . . Elizabeth Keckley wrote her narrative [*Behind the Scenes*] after the Civil War. Emancipation had made an anti-slavery focus unnecessary and undesirable. In general, readers in the reunited states were more interested in healing wounds and moving toward a harmonious future than in rehearsing past wrongs that had divided and devastated their nation. Like other postbellum narrators, then, Keckley modified the tone and the interpretation of her story of life in bondage. She, as they, chronicled the atrocities and deprivations engendered by that system, but reinterpreted this suffering and degradation as a historical moment necessitated by the brief reign of evil in a land that was intended for better purposes. Like other postbellum slave narrators, Keckley justified the slaves' suffering as God's way of instructing His people. This did not mean that these writers neglected to catalog examples of the cruelty, capriciousness, and dehumanization of that institution or that they did not emphasize the contagion that deformed or destroyed everyone who came near it. But after the war, the South was less often depicted as a prison house or a contemporary Egypt from which a Moses must arise and lead his people to freedom. Slavery was reinterpreted as if wilderness experience and the chosen people were all those of the United States, whose sins of doubt and indecision that had allowed the evil forces to gain control had to be punished by this woeful period. Slavery, national division, the war itself were all necessary for the instruction and correction of the nation. Job replaced Moses as a dominant symbol. Slavery had hurt everyone, but the slaves had suffered most, and by biblical example they knew that more pain meant more gain for those who had kept the faith. In Elizabeth Keckley's words, "A wrong was inflicted," but slavery was also the "fire of the crucible" and "the fire may inflict unjust punishment, but then it purifies and renders stronger the principle." She can "afford to be charitable," she says, because "I was a feeble instrument in His hands, and through me and the enslaved millions of my race, one of the problems was solved that belongs to the great problems of human destiny."

ATTAINING THE AMERICAN DREAM

Such a reinterpretation could be seen as excessively charitable, accommodating, or even fatalistic, but it is more appropriately evaluated as subversively ennobling. Responsibility for slavery was transferred to higher planes and the heroism of the slaves was magnified. Slaves had been agents of cosmic truth, sacrificial lambs who became the means for national redemption. As the chosen instrument of a divine omnipotence, their importance was crucial, while slavery was revealed as a demonic moment and the authority of their masters was deflated. The slave protagonists could be portrayed in more heroic terms, as people whose survival bore witness to the ultimate power of Good, whose special sufferings had earned them special rewards, whose rise would be all the more stellar because of the depths from which they have traveled. The postbellum protagonist could be characterized as the epitome of the American Dream, surpassing Benjamin Franklin's rise from poverty to power by moving from being property to becoming proprietors. In Elizabeth

Keckley's case, she had gone from being a slave girl, repeatedly told she would never be worth her salt, to become a modiste and friend to Washington's political elite, the indispensable designer, the stage manager for the roles played by the families of the Confederate and the Union presidents.

In consenting to write her autobiography, Elizabeth Keckley believed she could again be the means by which a major wrong could be righted. She had been behind the scenes and knew the truth that could set her free. Her testimony could correct misunderstandings and promote positive actions. But her social position and the story that she had to tell required rhetorical structures and language for which there were not yet existing models. The postbellum slave narrative provided useful elements, but as a woman and a mother Keckley had experienced pressures and problems unreported by male slave writers. The manner and moments of her assertion and triumph were different from those of male slaves. In the cases where her defiance or her victories did resemble theirs, her violation of gender restrictions could work against her. Keckley's text was to the postbellum slave narratives as Harriet Jacobs's had been to slave narratives of the antebellum period. It could be accommodated within the basic structure of the genre but that genre needed modification to fit the form of female experience.

As the preceding discussion has shown, the antebellum elements restricted the usefulness of the model that Harriet Jacobs devised, but parts of that were useful also. The circumstances of the two women were similar enough to allow Keckley to adopt several of Jacob's strategies. Keckley, too, intended to write across the color line and, therefore, could anticipate an audience dominated by women readers willing to concede their ignorance about her subject but not to accept easily the authority of her rendition. And, like Harriet Jacobs, Elizabeth Keckley's determination to tell the truth required her to confess to incidents that could destroy her credibility and negate her claims to sisterhood. For example, she too felt compelled to report that she had been sexually harassed by a white man. In her case, Keckley had been unable, or unwilling, to confound her nemesis by choosing another, but she does not claim to have been raped. Indeed, her self-characterization and the abrupt, brief, and vague manner in which she relates that incident suggest otherwise. While she doesn't dwell on the sexual dilemma as Jacobs did, Keckley too refused to be labeled a victim or judged a criminal for having conceived a child without benefit of marriage. In fact, Keckley politicizes the question and disenfranchises the women as adequate jurors even more sharply than did Jacobs. The subject is one "fraught with pain," she says, and she chooses not to dwell upon it. But the only opinion that truly matters to her is that of her child and the implication here is that were it not for society's ill-advised reactions, he would not have cause for discomfort. "If my poor boy ever suffered any humiliating pangs on account of birth, he could not blame his mother, for God knows that she did not wish to give him life; he must blame the edicts of that society which deemed it no crime to undermine the virtue of girls in my then position."

Both authors wrote of selected incidents in their lives, choosing from their histories those moments they deemed most significant to their authorial enterprises. And both confronted the issues of authority and authenticity in the preface. Keckley begins, as does Jacobs, by conceding that her narrative might seem like fiction to some and asserting the truthfulness of her statements by confessing that she has not told the entire truth. "My life, so full of romance, may sound like a dream to the matter-of-fact reader, nevertheless everything I have written is strictly true; much has been omitted, but nothing has been exaggerated" was Keckley's version. In these and other ways, Elizabeth Keckley's *Behind the Scenes* resembles Harriet Jacobs's *Incidents in the Life of a Slave Girl*. But its differences are critical.

DEPARTING FROM JACOBS'S MODEL

Some are fairly subtle and were it not for the effect of them in aggregate, could be attributed to differences of personality ~~ ~ublishing prerogative. For example, Elizabeth Keck- ⸽ call upon another individual to authenticate or ⸽ ⸽ her narrative. Elizabeth Keckley assigns to herself t that Lydia Maria Child played in Jacobs's text, abso⸽ ⸽acobs for any possible "indecorum" in discussing "delicate subjects" and "willingly tak[ing] the responsibility for presenting them with the veil withdrawn." But Elizabeth Keckley matter-of-factly declares "In writing as I have done, I am well aware that I have invited criticism; but before the critic judges harshly, let my explanation be carefully read and weighted." And a few pages later she writes, "It may be charged that I have written too freely on some questions, especially in regard to Mrs. Lincoln. I do not think so; at least I have been prompted by the purest motive." Clearly she relies less on the mask of polite deference or strategic withdrawal than did Harriet Jacobs with her "Pity me and pardon me, O virtuous reader, but . . ." approach. Keckley's assumption of equality, indeed her authority to instruct and to correct is made quite clear by the end of her preface when she writes

> I do not forget, . . . that ladies who moved in the Washington circle in which [Mary Lincoln] moved, freely canvassed her character among themselves. . . . If these ladies could say anything bad of the wife of the President, why should I not be permitted to lay her secret history bare, especially when that history plainly shows that her life, like all lives, has its good side as well as its bad side? None of us are perfect, for which reason we should heed the voice of charity when it whispers in our ears, "Do not magnify the imperfections of others."

Keckley's narrative stance not only demonstrates a difference between two individual women writers, it also suggests that in the postbellum era, women could claim a greater freedom for themselves and their literature. Before the war, they generally found it strategically helpful to present themselves as long-suffering and nonviolent victims of oppression. For example, Harriet Jacobs needed to persuade her readers that slaves were women and sisters and that as women they could and should extend more than their sympathies to them. Therefore, she offered a more radical alternative to the True Womanhood construct, but she also downplayed the slave women's abilities to help themselves, chose incidents common to domestic fiction, and modulated her tone to effect the greatest sympathy and strongest support. They and she were as ladylike as possible. Linda Brent used sass and manipulation in resourceful and generally effective ways, but when slapped or pushed, she screamed, trembled, or fainted. Elizabeth Keckley, on the other hand, was freer to describe physical confrontation and resistance. Both antebellum and postbellum whites might consider it unseemly for a black or a woman to raise a hand against a white man, but the heroism of both during the Civil War made postbellum readers a bit more inclined to tolerate, excuse, perhaps even admire, a black woman's desperate attempts to defend her virtue and to preserve her pride by any means necessary.

Elizabeth Keckley included an incident when she physically defended herself. Here again was the image of the black woman betrayed by her white sister, for it was Mrs. Burwell, a "morbidly sensitive" and "helpless" woman, who urged the local schoolmaster to subdue Keckley's "Stubborn pride." As Keckley describes the situation, it was not the undeserved beating that precipitated her violent reaction. It was this man's refusal to respect her as a woman. Mr. Bingham instructed her to take down her dress and Keckley in a direct address to her readers says: "Recollect, I was eighteen years of age, was a woman fully developed, and yet this man cooly bade me take down my dress." Such an indignity was not only intolerable but justified further defiance, and she continued, "I drew myself up proudly, firmly, and said: 'No, Mr. Bingham, I shall not take down my dress before you. Moreover, you shall not whip me unless you prove the stronger. Nobody has a right to whip me but my own master, and nobody shall do so if I can prevent it.'" Here clearly she restricts the grounds of grievance. She continues to address him as "Mr. Bingham" and she does not challenge the male prerogative to discipline females who show too much spirit. She does, however, refuse to submit herself to the view or abuse of a man who has not legal claim to her body. Though she fought vigorously, she was brutally beaten. Moreover, her adherence to social mores was not rewarded, for when she reported her abuse to her master and insisted that he justify his failure to protect her, he picked up a chair and knocked her down. Keckley continued to display self-respect and they continued to try to destroy it. She won. Her resorting to physical defense compelled the men to abandon their rope and rawhide and to snatch chairs, sticks, brooms, and whatever they could to subdue her. In resorting to such weapons, they abdicated the symbols of power and authority. Instead of inflicting punishment and discipline, they were humiliating and defeating themselves.

Keckley carefully showed that her violence was a reaction of extreme desperation and that each of her transgressors came to repent and to pay for their sins. She does not present the confrontations and the victory as purely personal episodes. After Mr. Bingham's third attempt to conquer her spirit, Keckley reports, "As I stood bleeding before him, . . . he burst into tears, and declared that it would be a sin to beat me any more. My suffering at last subdued his hard heart;

he asked my forgiveness, and afterwards was an altered man. *He was never known to strike one of his servants from that day forward"* (emphasis added). And just as important as the divine intervention that caused the schoolmaster (and eventually the minister and his wife) to repent was the solidarity of the community. For Keckley's self-respect could not allow her to submit passively to unjustified brutality, but she chose to limit her violence to self-defense. Revenge was not a motive, but justice was her due. It was not enough that the men stop abusing her, and she writes that "These revolting scenes created a great sensation at the time, were the talk of the town and neighborhood, and I flatter myself that the actions of those who had conspired against me were not viewed in a light to reflect much credit upon them." Since it is unlikely that the men took it upon themselves to spread the news of their confrontations, one must conclude that Keckley herself reported it. The victory then was a common one. The good whites joined the aggrieved blacks and forced the transgressors to desist. The analogy to postbellum readers was clear.

CHRONICLING THE ACHIEVEMENTS OF THE EX-SLAVE

Descriptions of physical resistance such as this one were fairly common in postbellum narratives. However, they were carefully contextualized to avoid arousing fears among whites. Whites in the postbellum period may have been slightly more tolerant toward slave rebels, but even with the care taken to assuage their fears of violent reprisals, the enormous number of newly freed slaves caused them considerable concern. Again, Elizabeth Keckley's narrative demonstrates how many writers responded. Unlike the antebellum slave narrators who downplayed their individual initiative and self-discipline to enhance their argument against the insidiousness of slavery as an institution, postbellum narrators needed to convince their readers that the former slaves, especially those who had passively endured their bondage, were capable of assuming the responsibilities of freedom.

This was partly accomplished by increasing the length of time that the narratives covered. Although many antebellum narratives were written years after the authors had escaped from slavery, most climaxed with their arrival in the free North. Postbellum narratives, by contrast, normally went beyond that arrival to describe the actual or anticipated achievements of the former slave. From one perspective, to depict life in slavery as a character-building experience or as one very difficult preparatory school which developed the skills and courage to go on to bigger and better things might seem to be excessive, naive, or far too accommodating. Keckley's story is actually more that of an ambitious and calculating hero who is recounting the cost of her success and impressing the value of her achievements upon others who were inclined to underestimate it. She made it clear that from her childhood she was industrious and ambitious to prove herself worth her salt. At age four, she cherished her appointment as a nursemaid because it was a way to leave the rude cabin and move into the master's house. While such desires could have been as childish as simply wanting better food and warmer quarters, they also show the early stages of the personal attributes that would move her into the White House. Her story testified not simply to her own strength of character but it represented the strength and courage that enabled her fellow slaves to emerge from the crucible, and it typified that of other black achievers whose autobiographical offerings would follow her model. In this way, *Behind the Scenes* is a prototype for later black success stories such as *Elizabeth, A Colored Minister of the Gospel, Born in Slavery* (1889), *From the Virginia Plantation to the National Capitol; or, The First and Only Negro Representative in Congress from the Old Dominion* (1894) by John Mercer Langston, *From Slave Cabin to the Pulpit: The Autobiography of Reverend Peter Randolph: The Southern Question Illustrated and Sketches Of Southern Life* (1893), and Booker T. Washington's *Up from Slavery* (1901).

As is evident from their titles, the emphasis upon black achievement in these works was manifest before the first incident in the life of a former slave was related. Authorship, integrity, transcendence, authority, and authenticity are equally important. In Keckley's case, her declaration of authorship interrupts the title and subtitle and makes a single statement of integrity, authority, and transcendence. Equally spaced on the title page are "Behind the Scenes," "by Elizabeth Keckley, formerly a slave, but more recently modiste, and friend to Mrs. Abraham Lincoln," and "Or, Thirty Years a Slave, and Four Years in the White House." "By Elizabeth Keckley, formerly a slave" is in the tradition of "Phillis Wheatley, servant to . . ." and "Frederick Douglass, an American Slave." But while it immediately and prominently identifies its author with slavery, *Behind the Scenes* also modifies that form by stressing a movement up from slavery. Keckley's identification as "formerly a slave, but more recently modiste, and friend" and her juxtaposition of "Thirty Years a Slave, and Four Years in the White House" rejects a static definition as "slave" or even "former slave." It suggests progressive movement, and it emphasizes the social distance traveled. . . .

Before she wrote *Behind the Scenes,* Elizabeth Keckley had enjoyed a reputation, particularly within the black community, as a lady of impeccable taste and high standards. She had created a thriving business and had earned access to the homes and confidences of the wives of the Washington power elite. Because it was well known that both the president and the First Lady were subject to her influence, prominent people from all races sought her support for their projects. She numbered among her personal friends and acquaintances Frederick Douglass, Henry Highland Garnet, Martin Delany, several congressmen, and other successful African American women including the twelve black school teachers in the District of Columbia system. Elizabeth Keckley was an active member of and a generous financial contributor to the Fifteenth Avenue Presbyterian Church where, it is reported, her manner was so dignified and her attire so grand that many worshipers arrived early in order to witness the arrival of the woman they knew as "Madame Keckley." According to her minister and friend, the Reverend Francis Grimke, hers was a genuine piety. In his eulogy he named her "a true child of God. She loved the Lord Jesus Christ in sincerity and truth." And, Grimke also reports, "She was a woman who thoroughly respected herself. . . . She had a high sense of what was befitting, and held herself up to it, and held others up to it also." Madame Keckley knew that she was a witness to and a participant in historic occasions and that she had become an example and an exemplar. She cherished her reputation for its personal vindication of her against a former mistress who predicted that Keckley would never "be worth her salt." She was gratified that her achievements were viewed as inspiration for other blacks and as proof of racial progress to whites. It was her sense of history, her piety, and her pride that made her decide to write *Behind the Scenes* at the time and in the manner that she did.

CHAPTER 2

The Slave Narrative's Literary Sources

Slave
Narratives

The Slave Narrative and the Puritan Captivity Narrative

Richard Slotkin

Richard Slotkin is the author of *Regeneration Through Violence: The Mythology of the American Frontier, 1600–1860* and other works on America's frontier experience. In this excerpt from *Regeneration Through Violence,* Slotkin draws parallels between the Puritan captivity narrative, one of the most popular literary genres during America's formative years, and the slave narrative. According to Slotkin, the circumstances of the slave held in bondage call to mind those of the Puritan held in captivity by Native Americans. Using Josiah Henson's slave narrative as an example, Slotkin shows that the narrator of the Puritan captivity narrative and the narrator of the typical slave narrative record similar experiences. Slotkin then goes on to show how Harriet Beecher Stowe used the slave captivity narrative in creating *Uncle Tom's Cabin.*

Perhaps the most significant use of the captivity mythology was in the narratives of southern slavery published by the abolitionists between 1830 and 1860. These narratives were largely personal accounts by escaped or freed former slaves, some of them genuinely autobiographical, some fictional, some the result of collaboration between the former slaves and white abolitionists. Given this variety of auctorial characters, the consistency of the narrative pattern from account to account is remarkable. The black slave undergoes the classic captivity. He (or she) is born with a natural predisposition to Christian meekness, humility, and charity that, in Puritan times, would surely have been taken as a sign of indwelling grace and marked him as elect [worthy of entrance

Excerpted from Richard Slotkin, *Regeneration Through Violence: The Mythology of the American Frontier, 1600–1860.* Copyright © 1973 Richard Slotkin. Reprinted with permission from the author.

into heaven]. The slave's circumstances, however, make it impossible for this Christian soul to realize itself. The slave system denies him (in most cases) the full benefits of "instituted worship," subjects him to the lusts and whims of a worldly master, and perverts his loyalty and willingness to work into the brutality of the overseer and the "laziness" and "carelessness" of the forced laborer. Like the white Puritan captive to Indians, the slave is in an alien environment, a Christian in hell. If he succeeds in hell's terms, he becomes like the devils around him (like the white-Indian renegade). If he fails, by being "shiftless," "thievish," or "careless," he falls into habits that any exponent of the Protestant ethic must regard as evil and in that way shares the devil's nature. There is nothing he can do but escape or "be redeemed" from his captivity.

The escape is often accompanied or preceded by a religious conversion. Discovering the sweetness of Christ, the slave perceives his master's distance from the white man's ostensible Christianity and recognizes his own sinfulness in cooperating with, admiring, and emulating his white master. In one of the best of these accounts, *Father [Josiah] Henson's Story of His Own Life,* this sense of sin—the necessary precondition for Puritan conversion—is accentuated by the fact that Henson has served as an overseer and, in an attempt to "be like his master," has prevented some of his fellow slaves from attaining freedom. Revulsion from sin frees the black soul of its spiritual bondage to slavery; the aid of Christian men frees his body as well; and the redemption of the soul is followed by the rescue of the body, as in the classic captivity of Mary Rowlandson. True to the pattern, the narrative ends with the reunion of the family group sundered by captivity.

In this slave-captivity narrative, the contemporary characters of black man, southerner, and abolitionist take on the mythic disguises of seventeenth- and eighteenth-century captivities. The black, like Mrs. Rowlandson and her fellows, is passive under the sufferings of exile, enforced servitude, and the rupture of the family. Father Henson, whose mother is sold away from him, accepts the tragedy as part of his lot and tries to be a "good nigger." The captive's and the slave's heroism is internal: they become true Christians under the stress of un-Christian circumstances. Physical rescue is an adjunct of this spiritual rescue and is most often effected, not by the captive's strength or intelligence, but by the power of an outside, semidivine agency. Father Henson frankly avows a sense of pride in his skill and courage, which enabled him first to make his escape from the South and then to return and aid other slaves to escape. Harriet Beecher Stowe, who based the character of Uncle Tom on Henson, found it necessary to eliminate this quality of Henson's character in order to make her protagonist more perfectly an embodiment of the Christian values of American society—values that had traditionally been embodied in the figure of the white female captive. She embodies the militant aspect of Henson in the figure of George Harris, whose pride and willingness to shoot his way to freedom are morally suspect and are rebuked both by the pacifism of the Quakers on the underground railroad and by the sentimental pleas of his Christian wife, Eliza.

THE CAPTIVITY NARRATIVE AND *UNCLE TOM'S CABIN*

Uncle Tom's Cabin acquires much of its force from its ironic inversions of the classic captivity-narrative situation, in which the dark people captivate the white. Nonetheless, it preserves the structures and moral biases of that mythology intact. The admirable qualities of Tom are those of the captive: passivity, persistence in Christianity in the face of torment, charity, sympathy, purity. As Mrs. Rowlandson moved from the mild bondage to vanity (in Lancaster) to a vision of the explicit bondage of her soul to sin (in the Indian camp), so Tom moves from the gentle servitude of Kentucky to the more drastic slavery of the Deep South. His qualities of character are, as William R. Taylor notes, "feminine" qualities, as these were seen in the literature of nineteenth-century America; and the archetypal protagonist of the captivity was either actually or symbolically female. Thus Wendell Phillips reports that at an abolition meeting a former slave failed to rouse the enthusiasm of the crowd until he had evoked an image of a black mother being whipped for protecting her child; and pictures and anecdotes in antislavery journals dwelt upon the persecution of female slaves in images and language which echo the captivity literature of the Mathers [Puritan ministers Increase and his son, Cotton].

The masculine qualities of intelligence, lust for power, strength, and the will and capacity to exploit are, in Mrs. Stowe's novel, the attributes of whites—not, as in the captivity myths, the attributes of "darks." George Harris is proud and violent because of his white blood and white appearance; Tom is described as a "pure African." The quintessential character of the white male exploiter is that of Simon Legree, a planter whose style of life and manners are those of a Simon Suggs or Sut Lovingood, whose ancestry is sharp-dealing Yankee, and whose current status is that of slave driver—in short, a figure who combines all the evils of exploitive commerce, as these were perceived in New England. Significantly, Legree shares the characteristic attributes of the most evil figures in the captivity narratives. He is a monster of sensuality, with a craving for miscegenation; he is lazy, living by the labor of captives and women; he devotes his time to pleasure, profligacy, and hunting.

There are good planters as well as bad, but their goodness arises from their sharing the nature and, to some extent, the situation of the captive. Thus St. Clare is seen as an unwilling captive of the slave system, bound to it by spiritual weakness. As a man, he is more effeminate in his helplessness than Uncle Tom and therefore is still more to be pitied, according to the standards of the captivity myth.

The spectrum of southern character and motivation, both black and white, is reduced in this novel to the presanctioned, simple types of the captivity mythology. The real slave's complex motives for acquiescing in and rebelling against slavery, as expressed by Father Henson, are reduced in Uncle Tom to the ineluctable image of captive feminine Christianity. The slaveowner appears either as the white-Indian Legree . . . , the courtier-gone-native Alfred St. Clare . . . , or the enervated Augustine St. Clare. . . .

Mrs. Stowe's use of the captivity mythology is, however, not self-conscious. . . . Her falling into the idiom of the captivity myth—and her audience's response to that idiom—is apparently unconscious and characteristic. That this coincidence of mind between audience and propagandist significantly contributed to the success of abolitionist propaganda seems clear. But the success of the captivity myth in abolitionist tracts had its ill consequences as well, reinforcing as it did the tendency toward stereotyping of sectional characters and the oversimplification of the South's problem. The captivity myth's terms contained a pattern for solving that problem which was to prove ultimately destructive of the ends of abolitionism.

Frederick Douglass's Use of Abolitionist Documents

John W. Blassingame

John W. Blassingame is the editor of *Slave Testimony: Two Centuries of Letters, Speeches, Interviews, and Autobiographies* and the author of *The Slave Community: Plantation Life in the Antebellum South* and other books on American slavery. In this excerpt from his introduction to *The Frederick Douglass Papers*, Blassingame identifies some of the sources that Frederick Douglass used when he authored *Narrative of the Life of Frederick Douglass, an American Slave.* According to Blassingame, Douglass relied extensively on abolitionist newspapers and on a book published by Theodore Weld in 1839 titled *American Slavery As It Is*, which, through slaves' stories, advertisements for runaway slaves, and other documents, highlighted the hardships of life under slavery. Douglass also used the oral narratives of slaves whom he met on the abolitionist lecture circuit.

Although the *Columbian Orator* was [Frederick] Douglass's key textbook during the time of his enslavement in Maryland, his central texts once he escaped from slavery were abolitionist newspapers, magazines, books, and pamphlets and slave narratives. Such works greatly expanded his knowledge of autobiographies. In abolition sources alone, Douglass read dozens of narratives of fugitive slaves before he sat down to write his autobiography in 1844.

Between 1838 and 1844 Douglass avidly read such anti-slavery publications as the *Liberator, National Anti-Slavery Standard, Liberty Bell, Emancipator, Anti-Slavery Almanac,* and *American and Foreign Anti-Slavery Reporter* that contained speeches, interviews, and autobiographies of dozens

Excerpted from John W. Blassingame, "Introduction to Volume One," in *The Frederick Douglass Papers*, edited by John W. Blassingame, John R. McKivigan, and Peter P. Hinks. Copyright © 1999 Yale University. Reprinted with permission from Yale University Press.

of fugitive slaves including Lunsford Lane, James Curry, Lewis Clarke, and the *Amistad* rebels. Equally significant, the abolition newspapers and magazines published reviews of the autobiographies of blacks and whites and furnished Douglass with further advice on the elements of the proper autobiography. At a very early period, Douglass also came to know the "slave's biographer," Isaac T. Hopper, who published a long-running popular column of slave narratives in the *National Anti-Slavery Standard* under the heading "Tales of Oppression."

DOUGLASS'S USE OF *AMERICAN SLAVERY AS IT IS*

Another source of information about the autobiographical canon that Douglass read repeatedly was Theodore Dwight Weld's *American Slavery As It Is.* Douglass quoted frequently from Weld's work in the speeches he gave between 1841 and 1845. Indeed, *American Slavery As It Is* long represented for Douglass the standard by which to measure all statements about the character of America's peculiar institution. The book was, Douglass wrote in 1853, the "repository of human horrors."

Douglass relied so extensively on personal narratives in *American Slavery As It Is* that they undoubtedly formed the structure, focus, and style of his *Narrative.* He learned, for instance, that most of the accounts that Weld published followed letters vouching for the author's integrity and veracity. Weld himself repeatedly stressed the importance of a truthful portrayal of slavery, urged witnesses to "speak what they know, and testify what they have seen," and commanded them to demonstrate a "fidelity to truth." Conscious of the incredulity of his northern readers, Weld insisted on making a clear distinction between opinion and fact: "Testimony respects matters of *fact,* not matters of opinion: it is the declaration of a witness as to *facts,* not the giving of an opinion as to the nature or qualities of actions, or the *character* of a course of conduct."

American Slavery As It Is may also have played a crucial role in Douglass's original decision to write and publish his *Narrative.* Significantly, in a prefatory "Note" to his book, Weld announced that the American Anti-Slavery Society intended to publish other "TRACTS, containing well authenticated facts, testimony, personal narratives, etc. fully setting forth the *condition* of American slaves." Each prospective author unknown to the Executive Committee of the Society had to furnish references. Weld specified exactly the kinds of narratives in which the society had an interest:

> Facts and testimony respecting the condition of slaves, *in all respects*, are desired; their food, (kinds, quality, quantity), clothing, lodging, dwellings, hours of labor and rest, kinds of labor, with the mode of exaction, supervision, &c.—the number and

HARRIET JACOBS'S USE OF THE DOMESTIC NOVEL

The female domestic novel of the mid-nineteenth century was a source for Harriet Jacobs as she wrote Incidents in the Life of a Slave Girl. *Jacobs wrote the autobiography under the name Linda Brent.*

Linda Brent's *Incidents in the Life of a Slave Girl* suggests how autobiography failed to meet the female slave's attempt to express her self or to discover her self. Brent, in fact, found the genre so wanting that she fled it—and ran straight to the arms of the more usable, more female domestic novel. . . .

Maturity for a nineteenth-century woman required three victories: control of her own chastity; attainment of a successful marriage; and ability at marriage and mothering of her own children. Only those women who achieved success in these three areas—that is, women who remained virgins until their triumph as wives and mothers—were enviable women, female adults. As a slave, from the start, Brent possessed no opportunities for these victories. She could not be a successful woman, in white terms, any more than [Frederick] Douglass could be a successful man. . . . And, like Douglass's, Brent's narrative centers around her attempt to gain the virtues of adulthood, as it is defined by the white culture. . . .

Why then did she choose the domestic novel as a means of ordering her autobiography? The answer is, I think, simple. She gains much by making the form her own. First of all, the form is hers, by the right of the traditions of gender, and in accepting it, she places herself in the community of women so well defined in the nineteenth century. . . . Secondly, the form itself gives her what the culture has taken away—a means to assert her own righteousness and, in female terms, class. By writing in the form of the domestic novel, she, a black woman, asserts her desire to be chaste; thus, she establishes her kinship with other women, white and black. At once, she is like them.

Annette Niemtzow, "The Problematic of Self in Autobiography: The Example of the Slave Narrative," in *The Art of the Slave Narrative: Original Essays in Criticism and Theory.* Ed. John Sekora and Darwin T. Turner. Macomb: Western Illinois University Press, 1982, pp. 104–106.

times of meals each day, treatment when sick, regulations respecting their social intercourse, marriage and domestic ties, the system of torture to which they are subjected, with its various modes; and *in detail*, their *intellectual* and *moral* condition. Great care should be observed in the statement of facts. Well-weighed testimony and well-authenticated facts, with a responsible name, the Committee earnestly desire and call for.

Given this note, it is probably no accident that the publisher Douglass chose for his first autobiography was the American Anti-Slavery Society and that he found two people, William Lloyd Garrison and Wendell Phillips, "personally known" to its executive committee to write prefatory notes to his *Narrative*.

DOUGLASS'S USE OF SLAVE NARRATIVES

Although the other autobiographical works Douglass read were probably somewhat less influential than *American Slavery As It Is*, they were no less significant. The most salient features of the slave narratives he read in the abolition press were their brevity, directness, simplicity, and lack of specificity. Often editors prefaced the accounts with declarations that publication had been delayed until the fugitive had reached Canada. Editors of the accounts of fugitives who remained in the United States frequently tried to guarantee their anonymity by giving them fictional names, deleting specific references to their masters and places of enslavement, or citing initials for all personal and place names that might possibly serve as keys to the real identity of the narrator. While helping to ensure the safety of the fugitive, such practices, the amanuenses realized, seriously undermined the credibility of the accounts. In many cases, however, the guarantee of anonymity was the sine qua non for obtaining accounts from frightened fugitives.

Significantly, Douglass had some of his first exposures to the narratives of fugitive slaves in oral rather than written form at the home of the most prolific of the slaves' amanuenses, Isaac T. Hopper. Reflecting in 1853 on his introduction to Hopper, Douglass asserted that he first saw him in September 1838 when Hopper was a witness in a fugitive slave case. In a review of Lydia Maria Child's biography of Hopper, Douglass discussed his "intimate acquaintance with the venerable, Quakerly gentleman" and his visits to Hopper's home in the early 1840s, where he "listened to some of the admirable stories and adventures in the matter of rescuing fugitives."

Biblical Allusion and Imagery in Frederick Douglass's *Narrative*

Lisa Margaret Zeitz

In this essay, Lisa Margaret Zeitz of the University of Virginia highlights Frederick Douglass's use of the Bible as a source for his first slave narrative, *Narrative of the Life of Frederick Douglass, an American Slave*. According to Zeitz, Douglass uses biblical language and metaphors throughout his narrative. Douglass makes such allusions to refute the widespread claim that Christianity sanctioned slavery and to draw a comparison between the crusade against slavery and the battle between good and evil that is the basis of so many situations in the Old and New Testaments. Zeitz compares Douglass to Christ and to the prophets of the Old Testament.

Frederick Douglass' *Narrative*, first published in 1845, has been described by a recent commentator as "a consciously literary work, and one of the first order." While I suspect that few readers would challenge this view, surprisingly few have sung the work's praises in the annals of literary criticism. Although pioneering discussions of Douglass' use of agrarian and animal imagery, nautical metaphors, ironic humour, and techniques which create verisimilitude have established a firm base upon which further studies may be built, there is one area of investigation in which the groundwork has yet to be laid. This is the whole subject of the role of religious language and Biblical allusion in the *Narrative*.

The use of Biblical references and imagery would not have seemed peculiarly "literary" or learned to men of Douglass' time. Knowledge of the Scriptures was "general," and an author's allusions to Christian concepts would have bolstered his readers' understanding, not interfered with it. The

Excerpted from Lisa Margaret Zeitz, "Biblical Allusion and Imagery in Frederick Douglass's Narrative," *CLA Journal*, vol. 25, pp. 56–64, June 1982. Reprinted with permission from the College Language Association.

white abolitionist audience for whom Douglass wrote the *Narrative* would certainly have responded to a language of religious reference, but Douglass was probably not consciously catering to their tastes. . . .

CHRISTIANITY AND SLAVES

Douglass uses Biblical phrasing primarily to refute the claim that Christianity sanctions slavery. He makes this strategy clear when he explains that "of all slaveholders . . . religious slaveholders are the worst." The case of Captain Auld is the most telling: he "experiences religion," and becomes a "much worse man after his conversion than before," having found "religious sanction and support for his slaveholding cruelty." In fact, the religious sanction is founded on a misreading of Scripture, as Douglass' example of such a passage shows. His master quotes the following as justification for beating a slave: "'He that knoweth his master's will, and doeth it not, shall be beaten with many stripes.'" The verse quoted appears in Luke xii, a chapter which focuses on the responsibilities of a Christian disciple. The "Master," Christ, exhorts his followers to seek the kingdom of heaven and to live in a state of constant readiness for that day when they will be judged, for they are "like unto men that wait for their lord." In the parable which follows, Christ develops this figure of man as servant; all who "wait, for their lord" must be prepared to meet him at any time, "for the Son of man cometh at an hour when ye think not." The servants of God may not postpone their preparations:

> But and if that servant say in his heart, My lord delayeth his coming; and shall begin to beat the menservants and maidens . . . [t]he Lord of that servant will come in a day when he looketh not for him, and at an hour when he is not aware, and will cut him in sunder, and will appoint him his portion with the unbelievers. And that servant, which knew his lord's will, and prepared not himself, neither did according to his will, shall be beaten with many stripes. (Luke xxi. 45–47)

It is clear from an examination of the Scriptural context that the slaveholder's Biblical "justification" for beating a slave is founded on a misreading of the Gospel. The slaveholder is exposed: *he* is the faithless servant who beats "menservants and maidens," and who, in turn, will be "beaten with many stripes" for failing to follow the commandments of the Lord of all. The words of the slaveholder have been turned back upon his own head, and he need fear both the Day of Judgment which is the end of time, and the Day of Judgment which will herald the death of the institution of slavery.

In the appendix to the *Narrative,* Douglass quotes extensively from Matthew xxiii, identifying Christianity in America with the worst excesses of the "ancient scribes and Pharisees." These quotations serve as excellent illustrations of the technique that identifies Biblical patterns operative in secular history. The passages selected emphasize the price to be paid by the oppressors: "'They bind heavy burdens, and grievous to be borne, and lay them on men's shoulders, but they themselves will not move them with one of their fingers. . . . But woe unto you . . . ye shall receive the greater damnation.'" The threatening voice of the prophet of social revolution is unmistakable.

The cursing of Ham, which some slaveholders insisted was proof of the justness of American slavery, is alluded to in the first chapter of the narrative. Douglass thus begins his account with a reference to that section of the Book of Genesis which was held by the enslavers to mark the beginning of black history. As Douglass proceeds to demonstrate, however, this "justification" of slavery is no longer "scriptural," for there are many slaves "who, like myself, owe their existence to white fathers, and those fathers most frequently their own masters." "If the lineal descendants of Ham are alone to be scripturally enslaved," Douglass argues, "it is certain that slavery at the south must soon become unscriptural." The very existence of slaves with white fathers "will do away the force of the argument, that God cursed Ham, and therefore American slavery is right." Douglass rejects the division of the human race into the enslaved (the descendants of Ham) and the enslavers, and advances, instead, the traditional Christian division of the race of man into the children of God and the children of the devil. In the lengthy quotation from Matthew xxiii in the appendix, that basic division appears in the explicit description of the Pharisees (whom Douglass has just identified with the "votaries" of "the Christianity of America") as "the child[ren] of hell." Douglass' citing of the term, "child of hell," is especially helpful in placing his prevalent use of such adjectives as "fiendish" and "infernal" within a Biblical context.

From the start Douglass associates the slaveholders with the forces of evil through his choice of traditional Christian terms for the demonic: the deeds of the slaveholders are "most infernal"; slavery itself is of an "infernal character"; "internal purpose," "infernal work," and "infernal grasp" all refer to the actions of the oppressors. "Fiendish" is another prevalent adjective, and, in what is perhaps the clearest illustration of Douglass' purpose in employing these traditional Christian terms for evil, the slave traders are described as "fiends from perdition" who "never looked more like their father, the devil."

Frederick Douglass

"None of them is lost," said Christ, "but the son of perdition." "He that committeth sin is of the devil. . . . Whosoever is born of God doth not commit sin. . . . In this the children of God are manifest, and the children of the devil." Mr. Plummer, Mr. Severe, and a "swarm of slave traders" are described as profane swearers; their blasphemy is further evidence of their sinfulness. Like their association with things "infernal" and "fiendish," the slaveowners' "bitter curses and horrid oaths" mark them as "children of the devil." It is these human demons who have brought about "the hottest hell of unending slavery."

Throughout the *Narrative* Douglass refers to his own brethren as "souls"; an explicit contrast is thus made between the genealogy of the slaveholders and that of the slaves, "children of a common Father." The scholars at Douglass' Sabbath school, for example, are "precious souls . . . shut up in the prisonhouse of slavery; their songs are the "prayer and complaint of souls boiling over with the bitterest anguish." The word "souls" emphasizes the slaves' humanity, their possession of that spark of divinity which animates an immortal being. The repetition of the term also draws attention to "the soul-killing effects of slavery." In contrast with the "souls" of the slaves are the "hardened hearts" of the enslavers. If any man needs to be convinced of the spirit-destroying effects of slavery, he has only to listen to the songs of Colonel Lloyd's prisoners and "analyze the sounds that shall pass through the chambers of his soul,—and if he is not thus impressed, it will only be because 'there is no flesh in his obdurate heart.'"

The Biblical passage alluded to here is from the Book of Ezekiel; the destruction of the wicked and God's offer of a new spirit to those who will abide by His laws are prophesied: "I will take the stony heart out of their flesh, and will give them an heart of flesh." As for those whose hearts remain obdurate, "I will recompense their way upon their own heads, saith the Lord GOD." Douglass is connecting his voice with the voices of the Old Testament prophets when he promises the coming destruction of the wicked. This strategy is used frequently in the *Narrative*.

Another instance of it is found in Douglass' description of his friend Nathan Johnson, "of whom I can say with a grateful heart, 'I was hungry, and he gave me meat; I was thirsty, and he gave me drink; I was a stranger and he took me in'." The passage quoted is Matthew xxv, 35, and once more the allusion invokes the Second Coming. Christ welcomes those who cared for their fellow men, though strangers, for they will inherit His kingdom: "Inasmuch as ye have done it unto one of the least of these my brethren, ye have done it unto me." Those who did not take in the needy stranger are cursed and sent into the "everlasting fire, prepared for the devil and his angels." As the gospel account alluded to makes clear, to reject the appeals of suffering humanity is to reject Christ Himself and, thus, Salvation. The passage provides further evidence of Douglass' use of Biblical allusion to strengthen his argument against the religious "sanctions" of slavery.

DOUGLASS AS A CHRIST FIGURE

The association of suffering humanity with Christ is used most effectively in the description of Douglass' fight with Mr. Covey, though this is not the only place where such a parallel is drawn. In chapter eight, for example, Douglass describes his fellow-slaves as "men and women of sorrow, and acquainted with grief"; in Isaiah the Lord is "a man of sorrows, and acquainted with grief." The slaves and their Lord are explicitly connected with each other. The same may be said of the description of the fight with Covey; Douglass is associated with Christ and Covey with Satan. The struggle thus stands representative of the perpetual battle between the children of God and the devil. Covey is called "the snake" by the slaves, and his defining characteristic is "his power to deceive," exactly that ability which is always associated with Satan. Douglass remarks ironically, "He seemed to think himself equal to deceiving the Almighty." Covey succeeds in "breaking" Douglass, but only for a short time. Before describing the battle that he calls "the turning-point" however, Douglass presents his famous account of the sailing ships on the Chesapeake Bay.

This account might aptly be seen as a kind of emblem for the overall movement of the *Narrative*. Framed between the description of Covey and the actual fight, and placed in the centre of the central episode, its position indicates its importance. Initially, "freedom's swift-winged angels" evoke utter despair and the anguished cry, "Is there any God? Why am I a slave?" But as Douglass thinks about the "protecting wing" of the sails, he vows that he will escape and that he will do so by water. We know from his later autobiographies that it was in the clothing of a sailor that he was delivered from bondage; his prophetic resolutions led him to freedom. The movement toward hope in the ship episode is emblematic of the movement of Douglass' life as it reaches its turning point: "There is a better day coming."

The struggle with Covey begins when Douglass loses consciousness in the fields. The overseer refuses to believe that he is unable to rise and strikes him on the head, leaving a large wound. Douglass runs, pushing through bogs and briers,

> barefooted and bareheaded, tearing my feet sometimes at nearly every step. . . . From the crown of my head to my feet, I was covered with blood. . . . My legs and feet were torn in sundry places with briers and thorns, and were also covered with blood.

Douglass' resemblance to the crucified Christ is unmistakable. When he finally confronts Covey again, he resolves to fight: "I seized Covey hard by the throat; and as I did so, I rose." His triumph is "a glorious resurrection, from the tomb of slavery, to the heaven of freedom." In 1841 Theodore Parker suggested that Christ must be seen as the "paragon of humanity": "There was never an age," he said, "when men did not crucify the Son of God afresh." Parker's remarks are especially illuminating when brought to bear on the parallel crucifixions and resurrections of the *Narrative;* so, too, are the words of St. Paul in the second epistle to the Corinthians: "As the sufferings of Christ abound in us, so our consolation also aboundeth by Christ." "As ye are partakers of the sufferings, so shall ye be also of the consolation."

For Douglass, consolation rests in the day of the destruction of slavery. Of Mr. Covey, the man who embodies the infernal, he says, "His comings were like a thief in the night." Once more, language turns back upon its surface meaning: In Paul's first epistle to the Thessalonians we find, "The day of the Lord so cometh as a thief in the night," and in the Second Epistle General of Peter, "The day of the Lord will come as a thief in the night." The day of the Lord is the Day of Judgment.

DOUGLASS THE PROPHET

The voice that speaks to us through this fabric of Biblical allusion is a prophetic voice. After each of three narrow escapes Douglass alludes to the famous Old Testament prophet Daniel, who was protected by the God he served: "I had escaped a worse than lion's jaws"; "I suppose I looked like a man who had escaped a den of wild beasts, and barely escaped them"; "I said I felt like one who escaped a den of hungry lions." In the Biblical account not only is Daniel saved, but those who had condemned him are cast into the pit where "the lions had mastery of them, and brake all their bones in pieces." Again the promise of the punishment of the wicked is alluded to.

Douglass aligns himself with one more prophet: Jeremiah. In the only true "vision" of the *Narrative*, he imagines the condition of his aged grandmother. She lives in utter loneliness, having been turned out to die; the children, "who once sang and danced in her presence, are gone," and she suffers in "the darkness of age." The vision concludes with the question, "Will not a righteous God visit for these things?" In the appendix to the *Narrative*, Douglass quotes the scriptural reference: "'Shall I not visit for these things? saith the Lord. Shall not my soul be avenged on such a nation as this?'"

The voice of the *Narrative* is that of the prophets of all ages. The apocalypse heralded is a fire of the soul, a spiritual liberation and resurrection which will lead to the day of actual physical freedom from slavery's chains. Douglass' work is a plea for action to his readers to take up "the sacred cause" that is truly sanctioned by Scripture, and hasten "the glad day of deliverance." The prophet has spoken, and who are we to doubt that "this good spirit was from God"?

The Slave Narrative and the Picaresque Tradition

Charles H. Nichols

Charles H. Nichols is the author of *Many Thousand Gone: The Ex-Slaves' Account of Their Bondage and Freedom*. In this essay, he draws a comparison between the slave narrative and picaresque novels such as *Lazarillo de Tormes*, a Spanish novel of the sixteenth century. The picaresque novel features a protagonist—the picaro—who is born in poverty and grows to adulthood as an outsider in his society and engages in a desperate struggle for survival that often involves stealing, using disguises, and becoming an outlaw. According to Nichols, slave narrators such as Frederick Douglass, William Grimes, Henry Bibb, and William Wells Brown resemble the picaro as they attempt to cope with and eventually escape from a life of bondage. Nichols claims that the picaresque novel and the slave narrative had fundamentally the same purpose: to undermine a corrupt society.

Early picaresque fiction like *Lazarillo de Tormes* and *Guzman de Alfarache*, have profoundly influenced the development of European fiction. It is not surprising, therefore, that there are illuminating parallels between Afro-American narrative modes and a work like *Lazarillo de Tormes*. In all these narrative forms we are struck by the self consciousness of the personality whose awareness seizes our attention. The early slave narratives, the autobiographies of Henry Bibb, or William Wells Brown, or Frederick Douglass or Josiah Henson present personae reminiscent of the picaro, Lazarillo. Like the Spanish "rogue," the slave narrators tell their life story in retrospect, after having triumphed over the brutalizing circumstances of their youth. William W.

Excerpted from Charles H. Nichols, "The Slave Narrators and the Picaresque Mode: Archetypes for Modern Black Personae," in *The Slave's Narrative*, edited by Charles T. Davis and Henry Louis Gates Jr. New York: Oxford University Press, 1985. Reprinted by permission of the Janklow & Nesbit Literary Agency on behalf of the copyright holder.

Brown and Frederick Douglass are internationally known orators and reformers. Josiah Henson has become the founder of a refugee colony and celebrated as Harriet Beecher Stowe's "Uncle Tom." Lazaro tells us that at the time he is writing, he has saved money and, having become his wife's pimp and the agent of the Arch priest of San Salvador, has become the town crier. The accounts they have given us of their lives as slaves, servants and scullery boys operate, therefore, on at least two levels of consciousness. In each account the writer presents a welter of realistic detail designed to drive home the brutality and inhumanity of his experience as a victim, a commodity, a rootless, alienated soul without hope or future. His origin is obscure, his masters heartless and treacherous. The episodic march of events in the narrative, its loose disregard of causality, its frequent use of coincidence and chance dramatize the chaos and decadence of the world here depicted. With bitter irony the picaro-slave underlines his contempt for the illusions, the chivalric pretensions and the folly of the master class. Spain in the sixteenth century is in decline; the *antebellum* South is in crisis. The servant sees his master's nakedness and human weakness as well as his power and wealth.

THE PICARO'S MASK

The other level of consciousness is the mask which a corrupt society and desperate need force on the picaro. Lazarillo's mother has offered her favors to a black slave in return for stolen food and firewood. Lazarillo becomes the servant of a blind master whose first act is to dash the boy's head against a stone statue. The boy escapes one vicious and niggardly master only to fall into the hands of another—a hypocritical and heartless priest. Similarly Lazarillo's connection with the idle and indigent squire or that consummate con-man, the pardoner, create in him a personality ruled by selfishness, deceit and trickery. The desperate jeopardy of his condition forces upon the servant-slave-picaro the urgency of his search for an identity, for survival. He looks out on the chaos and moral decay of a social order which denies his humanity. But being human the slave astonishes us by the ingenuity of his means of survival. "I was obliged," writes Lazarillo, "to draw upon my weakness for strength." Henry Bibb is more candid: "The only weapon of self defense that I could use successfully was that of deception."

The picaresque mode is therefore the achievement of a necessarily devious and subtle consciousness. The individual is engaged in a desperate struggle for survival; the ego rests on a shaky foundation. Like a trapped animal, the picaro is alert to every possible avenue of escape. His effective means of expression are comic modes—irony, satire, paradox, sarcasm, exaggeration, innuendo. He survives by stratagems; a trickster, he adopts protean roles—stage presence. For as [Ralph Waldo] Emerson wrote, "Surely no one would be a charlatan who could afford to be sincere!" Indeed as the tone and form of the genre develop in masters like Cervantes, Fielding or Mark Twain, the world of the picaro is characterized by an intriguing burlesque. The life of the ruling class is stripped of its pretensions in a wild masquerade. And the servant-trickster-con-man forces new kinds of perception on the reader. We are moved by a sense of compassion for the suffering individual; we cannot deny him some degree of spiritual triumph in his rise from bondage to freedom. What emerges is a many-colored light, fresh angles of vision, an epistemology which creates a dynamic awareness of the vital interaction of society's outcasts with powers whose religion, philosophy and claims to civilization seem vain indeed.

Lazarillo's whole consciousness is riveted on the problem of survival, for he is literally starving and homeless. Even when he attempts to serve his master faithfully he is subject to constant abuse. Nothing in his experience creates in him a sense of responsibility. Gil Blas was a valet; Moll Flanders, a felon and a prostitute with middle class ambitions.

The slave narrators are neglected (often abandoned) children constantly subject to physical punishment and hounded by fear. "I believed myself to have been cruelly wronged in some way, I could not clearly decide whether by the neighbors or by the world or by the laws of the land, and I became morose, quarrelsome and vengeful," writes Ralph Roberts. "Like Cain, my hand was against every man and every man's hand against me. I avoided much communication for several years with my fellow slaves and became careless and reckless." The isolation and deprivation of these slaves gave rise to an instability of personality which manifests itself in aggression, violence and superstition. They lose the capacity for love; the soul in them virtually dies. For the mental anguish of the picaro-slave is greater than his physical suffering. After being whipped, William Grimes wrote "It seems as though I should not forget this flogging when I die; it grieved my soul beyond the power of time to cure."

The slave's stratagems for survival, his ingenuity in playing out the roles his situation demanded is the leitmotif of the narratives. Henry Watson stowed away on a ship bound from Mississippi to Boston. Frederick Douglass escaped slavery in a sailor's uniform. Henry "Box" Brown was shipped by express from Richmond to Philadelphia. Ellen Craft dressed like a master travelling with his slave (her darker husband, William). Many ran literally hundreds of miles by night, hiding by day until they reached free territory. Some seized by uncontrollable rage whipped their overseers; a few plotted the murder of their oppressors. In short the picaresque mode with its accounts of "social disorder and psychic disintegration" creates one of the most popular forms of characterization in western fiction—the trickster, the rogue, the conman, the street man, the spy. And even the pattern of the early narrators carries us through the psychic underground and the brutality and absurdity of the modern city into the never-never land of fantasy toward which these battered souls yearn.

It is noteworthy that the slave narrators (like the protagonists of modern fiction) relentlessly examine their own motives and the psychological conflicts which their condition creates. Fear, hate, aggression and guilt stalk them all. And their moral and psychic regeneration—their attainment of manhood—is achieved by immense effort and staunch devotion to the ideals of personal freedom in a just society.

THE COMIC MODE

Such picaresque fiction as *Don Quixote, Candide,* and *Tom Jones* are satires, employing comic modes: exaggeration, innuendo, mistaken identity and ridicule. The slave narrative is rarely comic, but its personae have a curious double vision and a tendency to employ comic modes. Even the duller slaves perceived the irony of the slaveholders' loud boasts of a superior knowledge and love of liberty. While pretending to accept the religion which exhorted them to obedience, they embrace the God who delivered the Israelites from Egyptian bondage. Henry Bibb—a chronic runaway—had ready-made answers for patrols who might discover him in the woods. When asked what he was doing, he would be seeking a mare or a cow which had wandered off. "For such excuses I was let pass." William Wells Brown was sent by his irate master with a note and a dollar to be whipped by the town jailer. He cleverly gave the note and the money to another slave and sent him in his place. By fawning and deceit, William Hayden got unusual rewards for a slave. But when his master attempted to cheat him out of $300 he had paid for his freedom, he produced the papers and a pass his master had given him before witnesses and exposed the slaveholder's dishonest dealing. Josiah Henson writes of "midnight visits to apple orchards, broiling stray chickens, and first-rate tricks to dodge work." Henson wooed and won over his girl friends with his stolen "stray chickens." Far from feeling apologetic about stealing he felt it was his "training in the luxury of doing good . . . in the righteousness of indignation against the cruel and oppressive." And Frederick Douglass insisted that theft by a slave was only a question of *removal*—"the taking of his meat out of one tub and putting it in another. . . . At first he [the master] owned it in the *tub* and last he owned it in me." When Henry Bibb rode off on his master's donkey, he opined: "I well knew that I was regarded as property, and so was the ass; and I thought if one piece of property took off another, there could be no law violated in the act; no more sin committed in this than if one jackass had rode off another." Milton Clarke describes the slave, Aunt Peggy, who was a "master at stealing little pigs."

> With a dead pig in the cabin and the water all hot for scalding, she was at one time warned by her son that the Phillistines were upon her. Her resources were fully equal to the sudden emergency. Quick as thought, the pig was thrown into the boiling kettle, a door put over it, her daughter seated upon it, and a good thick quilt around her, the overseer found little Clara taking a steam bath for a terrible cold. The daughter, acting well her part, groaned sadly; the mother was busy in tucking in the quilt and the overseer was blinded, and went away without seeing a bristle of the pig.

The narrators' resistance to the slave system invariably manifests itself in subtle and ironic turns of speech. For they were conscious victims of a violent and rapacious society. The master exclaims angrily: "You scoundrel, you ate my turkey." The slave replies, "Yes, sir, Massa, you got less turkey but you sho' got mo' nigger." Peter Randolph tells of a slaveholder who dressed himself up for a fight and asked his favorite body servant how he looked:

"'Oh, massa mighty!' 'What do you mean by mighty, Pompey?' 'Why, Massa, you look noble.' 'What do you mean by noble?' 'Why, sir, you look just like a lion.' 'Why, Pompey, where have you ever seen a lion?' 'I seen one down in yonder field the other day, massa.' 'Pompey, you foolish fellow, that was a *jackass!*' 'Was it, Massa? Well, you look just like him.'"

As we have seen the picaresque tradition was often an attack on the chivalric ideal. The slave narrative performed the same function: it punctured the inflated rhetoric and empty boasts of the slavocracy. It destroyed the idyllic setting and cultivated a setting created by southern romance. It portrayed the rude and violent behavior of the master class and the inhumanity of the plantation system.

CHAPTER 3

Expressions of Freedom in the Slave Narrative

Slave
Narratives

Literacy and Freedom in the Slave Narrative

Janet Duitsman Cornelius

Janet Duitsman Cornelius, the author of *"When I Can Read My Title Clear": Literacy, Slavery, and Religion in the Antebellum South*, from which this essay is excerpted, explores the role of literacy in slaves' lives. According to Cornelius, literacy was, in many ways, a pathway to freedom for slaves. Literacy helped slaves like Frederick Douglass survive in a hostile environment, served as a mechanism for forming identity, and reinforced self-worth. Literacy was also "a communal act, a political demonstration of resistance to oppression and of self-determination for the black community." If Cornelius is correct in her assessment of the power of literacy on the antebellum plantation, then the slave narrative was a formidable weapon in the abolitionist crusade to eradicate American slavery.

The frequent hearing of my mistress reading the Bible aloud, . . . awakened my curiosity in respect to this *mystery* of reading, and roused in me the desire to learn. Up to this time I had known nothing whatever of this wonderful art, and my ignorance and inexperience of what it could do for me, as well as my confidence in my mistress, emboldened me to ask her to teach me to read. . . . In an incredibly short time, by her kind assistance, I had mastered the alphabet and could spell words of three or four letters. . . . [My master] forbade her to give me any further instruction . . . [but] the determination which he expressed to keep me in ignorance only rendered me the more resolute to seek intelligence. In learning to read, therefore, I am not sure that I do not owe quite as much to the opposition of my master as to the kindly assistance of my amiable mistress.

Frederick Douglass' moving description of how and why he learned to read while he was a slave is one of the best known and most popular sections of his famous autobiography. The compelling stories of people who were forbidden to learn to read and write and who risked punishment and death to learn forced nineteenth century readers to become aware of the cruelties of enslavement of human beings. Narratives written by escaped slaves in the antebellum United States almost always included "a record of the barriers raised against slave literacy and the overwhelming difficulties encountered in learning to read and write."

THE MEANING OF LITERACY

What did literacy mean to black people in slavery? Survival, according to Vincent P. Franklin, who points out that "education and literacy were greatly valued among Afro-Americans enslaved in the United States because they saw in their day-to-day experiences—from one generation to the next—that knowledge and information helped one to survive in a hostile environment." Literacy was a mechanism for forming identity, the freedom to become a person, according to James Olney. Olney finds significance in Douglass' conclusion to his narrative, which he ended with the words, "I subscribe myself . . . Frederick Douglass." According to Olney, "in that lettered utterance is assertion of identity and in identity is freedom—freedom from slavery, freedom from ignorance, freedom from non-being, freedom even from time," since writing endures beyond a moment or even beyond a lifetime.

Literacy also reinforced an image of self-worth: Lucius Holsey, who tried desperately to learn to read while an enslaved houseboy, "felt that constitutionally he was created the equal of any person here on earth and that, given a chance, he could rise to the height of any man," and that books were the path to proving himself as a human being. Milly Green's daughter recalled that Milly "was so proud of every scrap of book larnin' she could pick up" that she learned to read and write and that "atter de war was over she got to be a school teacher."

When African-Americans fought to gain literacy, they expressed a desire for freedom and self-determination which had deep roots in modern culture. The movement towards universal literacy and written culture is one of most important democratic developments in the modern world. While scholars of literacy recognize literacy's usefulness as a medium of social control and industrial training, the majority still agree that the basic result of literacy has been and is one of liberation. As Roger Chartier explains in his study of the beginning of universal written culture in the Renaissance, "personal communion with a read or written text liberated the individual from the old mediators, freed him or her from the control of the group, and made it possible to cultivate an inner life." The ability to read and write gave people the power to relate in new ways to one another and to authority. According to Harvey Graff, few in the modern world would question "the value of literacy for achieving fulfilling, productive, expanding, and participating lives of freedom."

For enslaved African-Americans, literacy was more than a path to individual freedom—it was a communal act, a political demonstration of resistance to oppression and of self-determination for the black community. Through literacy the slave could obtain skills valuable in the white world, thereby defeating those whites who withheld the skills, and could use those skills for special privileges or to gain freedom. Scholars of literacy have charted the impact a few literate people can make in a culture of illiterates; they serve as mediators and translators into a wider world for those who do not read. This ability to disperse knowledge from the larger world was a crucial act of resistance during slavery. Word of abolition movements, the writings of escaped slave Frederick Douglass, and John Brown's execution quickly spread through the slave quarters because they were passed on by those enslaved African-Americans who could read.

LITERACY MEANT ACCESS TO THE BIBLE

Literacy was also linked with freedom during slavery because it facilitated the African-American's creation of a liberating religious consciousness within the slave community. To be able to read the Bible was the first ambition of the converted illiterate Christian since, according to evangelical Protestantism, the individual should search the Scriptures in order to be saved. But the African-American used the Bible in an additional way, creating with its imagery a new reality from the slave experience. The ability to read the Bible, therefore, gave the reader the special mastery and control over this "sacred text" essential to leadership in the black church. African-Americans who could read were designated preachers by their own people as well as by whites; they were respected by black people as religious authorities because they held the key to the Bible without having to depend on whites to interpret Scriptures to them.

Traditional "Bible literacy" in the Western world emphasized the reception of the Word from authorities, so religious motives for learning to read are often considered passive, not liberating. For enslaved African-Americans, on the other hand, there was a "close relationship between religion and resistance." The African world view makes no distinction between the secular and the religious; spirituality is at the

FREEDOM AND LITERACY

In this excerpt from Narrative of the Life of Frederick Douglass, an American Slave, *Douglass explains that achieving literacy was his pathway to freedom.*

Very soon after I went to live with Mr. and Mrs. Auld, she very kindly commenced to teach me the A, B, C. After I had learned this, she assisted me in learning to spell words of three or four letters. Just at this point of my progress, Mr. Auld found out what was going on, and at once forbade Mrs. Auld to instruct me further, telling her, among other things, that it was unlawful, as well as unsafe to teach a slave to read. To use his own words, further, he said, "If you give a nigger an inch, he will take an ell. A nigger should know nothing but to obey his master—to do as he is told to do. Learning would *spoil* the best nigger in the world. Now," said he, "if you teach that nigger (speaking of myself) how to read, there would be no keeping him. It would forever unfit him to be a slave. He would become unmanageable, and of no value to his master. As to himself, it could do him no good, but a great deal of harm. It would make him discontented and unhappy." These words sank deep into my heart, stirred up sentiments within that law slumbering, and called into existence an entirely new train of thought. It was a new and special revelation, explaining dark and mysterious things, with which my youthful understanding had struggled, but struggled in vain. I now understood what had been to me the most perplexing difficulty—to wit, the white man's power to enslave the black man. It was a grand achievement, and I prized it highly. From that moment, I understood the pathway from slavery to freedom. It was just what I wanted, and I got it at a time when I the least expected it. . . . I set out with high hope, and a fixed purpose, at whatever cost, to learn how to read.

Frederick Douglass, *Narrative of the Life of Frederick Douglass, an American Slave,* 1845.

core of existence. Therefore it was through the black church, "the new religion of oppressed people," that resistance was fashioned. According to Margaret Creel, the religion shaped by enslaved African-Americans "offered a politic for collective consciousness and group conformation within an African-Christian synthesis." The African-American collective religious faith was "a progressive force and shield against white psychological and cultural domination." Their faith provided African-Americans with a will to create and the courage to persevere, helping them to remain spiritually free in spite of physical bondage. Former slaves recalled their determination to learn to read the Bible as an act of rebellion against white oppression.

Though some used their reading and writing skills to escape from slavery, few of the slaves who acquired literacy had illusions that literacy would immediately transform their lives. Their goals were more specific: slaves who learned to read and write could use literacy to gain advantages for themselves and mediate for their fellow slaves. Towards these ends, slaves used ingenuity and patience and risked discovery, death, and dismemberment to learn to read and write. . . .

LITERACY AND THE PRIVILEGED CLASSES

Reserving literacy for a privileged class is common in many cultures. In traditional India, for example, those who usurped the knowledge of Holy Writ reserved to Brahmans were punished by having hot oil poured into their mouths and into their ears. In traditional Tibet reading was taught by monks and possession of books was a sign of status. Medieval Europe similarly guarded the word. As late as the sixteenth century Henry VIII barred "all women other than gentle and noble women, together with artificers, journeymen, husbandmen, labourers, and servingmen of and under the degree of yeomen" from reading the Bible in English. However, white Southerners in the late eighteenth and early nineteenth century were in a unique position: they sought to prevent enslaved African-Americans from learning to read just as mass literacy was being vigorously promoted in England and in the northern United States as a positive good, necessary for training the citizens of a republic and for accustoming the population to industrial routine. Their defensiveness at being out of step made white Southerners increasingly adamant against literacy for their own enslaved working population.

Underlying this slaveowner defensiveness was the fear of a literate black population. Despite the protestations of the small group who would teach slaves that "Bible literacy" would uphold the social order, the majority of white Southerners knew better: they knew that knowledge was a two-edged sword which "could defend the social fabric or cut it to shreds." White Southerners were aware of the possibility that slaves who could read the Bible could also read David Walker's *Appeal* or *Freedom Journal*. In fact, the Bible itself was dangerous, as proven by Walker, Nat Turner, and others who used its messages of liberation to appeal for slave revolution. Opposition to those who would teach slaves never ceased in the antebellum period and advocates of slave literacy were confronted with the contradictions of their position.

Freedom Involves a Home and Family

Jean Fagan Yellin

Jean Fagan Yellin, a distinguished professor and scholar of African American literature, proved conclusively, in 1981, that Harriet Jacobs actually wrote her own story in *Incidents in the Life of a Slave Girl: Written by Herself.* According to the prominent African American scholar Henry Louis Gates Jr., "Few instances of scholarly inquiry have been more important to Afro-American studies than has Yellin's." In this excerpt from her introduction to *Incidents*, Yellin focuses on Jacobs's longing for a home of her own and her desire to protect her family from slavery's most severe aspects. In voicing these needs in her narrative, Jacobs represents many African American women held in bondage. For them, freedom did not only involve a dramatic escape to the North; freedom for slave women meant being able to play the role expected of nineteenth-century American women: establishing a home and raising a family.

In important ways, *Incidents [in the Life of a Slave Girl]* diverges from received notions about the slave narrative. This genre has been characterized as dramatizing "the quest for freedom and literacy." But *Incidents*, perhaps the most comprehensive slave narrative by an Afro-American woman, presents a heroic slave mother struggling for freedom and a home. She runs away to save her children—and particularly her daughter—from slavery. Men and women were valued for contrasting qualities in nineteenth-century America, and recent critics have pointed out that Frederick Douglass's classic 1845 *Narrative* presents its protagonist in terms of physical bravery, an important "masculine" attribute. It is not surprising that Jacobs presents Linda Brent in terms of motherhood, the most valued "feminine" role.

Much of Linda Brent's account of her triumphant battle for freedom as a "poor Slave Mother" does, however, follow patterns standard to the genre. As in other narratives, this struggle is seen as recurrent. Despite her escape from her master midway through the book and her flight north a dozen chapters later, she does not achieve her goal of freedom until the final pages. This pattern of repeated struggle is underscored by her efforts to free her children. While their purchase by their white father apparently rescues them from their mother's hated master, its questionable legality keeps them vulnerable to his demands. Because their father does not free them, although they are later sent to the North, they are not out of danger from seizure by their mother's young mistress until the end of the book.

FREEING THE FAMILY

The struggle for freedom is not only recurrent, it is ubiquitous. In *Incidents* one group of interpolated chapters discusses the attempts of Linda Brent's relatives—uncle, aunt, brother—to free themselves or their families. Another establishes a larger framework for their rebelliousness by discussing aspects of slave life in America, such as ideological indoctrination and religious practices, and by commenting on pertinent historical events such as the Nat Turner insurrection and the 1850 Fugitive Slave Law.

The resulting text is densely patterned. Although the slave narrator has been likened to the "rootless alienated" picaro [of picaresque literature], Jacobs's Linda Brent locates herself firmly within a social matrix, prefiguring twentieth-century views of the South by commentators as diverse as novelist William Faulkner and sharecropper Nate Shaw. Her recurrent efforts to free herself and her children are shown in the context of the attempts of successive generations of her family to free their children: her grandmother managed to emancipate one son; her father failed to free her brother or herself.

Linda Brent presents herself in relation to both racial groups that make up the closed society of the town, and she suggests the complex interrelationships connecting four generations of her grandmother's family and four generations of their masters. Checked against what we know of Jacobs's own life, this recital is remarkably accurate; most discrepancies involve not the narrator or her family—whose experiences cor-

*A slave couple on their wedding day. Many slaves felt that true
freedom came from establishing a home and raising a family.*

respond quite precisely to those of Jacobs and her family—but
whites. Linda Brent is inconsistent, for example, in citing the
age of her young mistress, and confuses the death of a minister's wife with the death of his parishioner.

Her grandmother's unusual status as a free woman with
powerful white friends provides important protection for
Linda Brent. It safeguards the house from marauding white
patrols after Nat Turner's rebellion; it gives Linda access to
the female slaveholder who tries to stop Dr. Flint from ha-
rassing her and to the one who temporarily shelters her; and
most important, it prevents Dr. Flint from raping her. Linda
Brent positions herself as "grandmother's child" not only in
relation to the white townspeople but also in relation to the
community of slaves and free blacks. Writing of prayer meetings and folk medicine, recounting tales and snatches of
songs, and describing festivities of the John Kuners—New
World celebrants of a transplanted African ceremony—she
records her involvement in black life.

In *Incidents* Linda Brent dramatizes her fight for freedom within the context of her family's active support. Despite terrible danger, grandmother, uncle, aunt, brother, even (she later learns) son and daughter—aid and abet her concealment and escape. Further, she presents her own efforts and those of her family within the larger configuration of an ongoing struggle for freedom by an entire black community. Charity's son James escapes, Luke runs from the speculator, Old Aggie is also hiding a runaway daughter. At crucial moments, the narrator identifies members of this larger community—Sally, Betty, and Peter—who support the family conspiracy on her behalf. After escaping north to Philadelphia, she quickly locates herself within a circle of black activists and searches for black migrants from her home town; later she repeats this pattern in New York, Boston, and Rochester.

Linda Brent's story is also different from most slave narratives in that its protagonist does not escape and quickly run north; almost a quarter of the book chronicles her years in hiding in the South. During that time, she is not solely occupied with reading and sewing. She uses her garret cell as a war room from which to spy on her enemy and to wage psychological warfare against him. From her cramped hiding place, she manipulates the sale of her children to their father, arranges for her daughter to be taken north, tricks her master into believing that she has left the South, and quite literally directs a performance in which Dr. Flint plays the fool while she watches, unseen.

LITERARY VICTORY

Incidents is a major slave narrative. It is also a major work in the canon of writings by Afro-American women. Harriet E. Wilson's *Our Nig* (1859), which modified formal aspects of slave narratives and women's fiction, transforming the black woman as fictional object into fictional subject, was "ignored or overlooked" by Wilson's "colored brethren"; only when it was reprinted in 1983 was its importance recognized. But *Incidents* was immediately acknowledged as a contribution to Afro-American letters.

Jacobs's book may well have influenced Frances Ellen Watkins Harper's pioneering novel *Iola Leroy; Or, Shadows Uplifted* (1892), which in turn helped shape the writings of Zora Neale Hurston and other foremothers of black women writing today. Like Jacobs, Harper worked in the South during Reconstruction. She located her book in that setting, and in a note to her novel she asserted that she wove "from threads of fact and fiction" her story about three generations of female "white slaves." *Iola Leroy* recalls *Incidents* not only in its focus on the struggle of a light-skinned woman who has been subjected to sexual abuse in slavery, but also in its choice of names and locations: Harper's characters representing the rich potential of black culture come from North Carolina, and their names are Harriet and Linda.

While Linda Brent's secondary goal—a home—remains elusive, *Incidents,* like all slave narratives, ends with the achievement of freedom, the narrator's primary goal. But even though her children, too, are free, Linda Brent's triumph is mixed. When her northern employer, Mrs. Bruce, offers to buy her in order to set her free, her relief is mingled with distress because her freedom is being achieved by purchase, a concession to slavery. Writing to Post, Jacobs likened her ordeal to the biblical models of Jacob and Job, expressing righteous outrage, then resignation: "I served for my liberty as faithfully as Jacob served for Rachel. At the end, he had large possessions; but I was robbed of my victory; I was obliged to resign my crown, to rid myself of a tyrant." Literary critics would dispute this. By creating Linda Brent, by writing and publishing her life story, Jacobs gained her victory.

The Slave Narrator as Antislavery Activist

Victor C.D. Mtubani

For many authors of slave narratives, the escape to freedom and authorship of their story did not conclude their work. These authors, Frederick Douglass being perhaps the best example, devoted themselves to the abolitionist cause after attaining their freedom. In this essay, Victor C.D. Mtubani, an historian of eighteenth-century England, outlines the abolitionist career of Olaudah Equiano after his release from slavery. Even before he wrote his narrative, *The Interesting Narrative of the Life of Olaudah Equiano*, published in 1789, Equiano "had become the recognized leader of the black community in Britain." He campaigned for the abolition of slavery and the slave trade and published essays and pamphlets to support those causes. His book was also a major contribution to the antislavery crusade in Great Britain.

The most articulate spokesman for the African cause, and by far the most widely travelled African living in England in the second half of the eighteenth century, was Olaudah Equiano (1745–1797), sometimes known as Gustavus Vassa, the African. Equiano had experience of Africa, having been born of Igbo stock in Nigeria. He was ten years old when he was captured and sold into slavery. He did not regain his freedom till 1766, when he was twenty-one years old. During that time he had travelled widely and had served two masters, Captain Pascal and Mr. Robert King. He had served Pascal during the campaigns of General Wolfe in Canada and Admiral Boscawen in the Mediterranean, during the Seven Years' War with France. He had made numerous voyages between America and the West Indies in the service of Robert King. He had visited England also several times while still

Excerpted from Victor C.D. Mtubani, "The Black Voice in Eighteenth-Century Britain," *Phylon: A Review of Race and Culture*, vol. 45.2, pp. 85–97, 1984. Reprinted by permission of *Phylon*.

Pascal's slave and even had been sent to school by Pascal's cousins, the Misses Guerin. After obtaining his freedom he had toured the Mediterranean, had been to the polar region on an expedition and had spent some time among the Mosquito Indians of South America as an assistant to an English doctor. The main concern of this paper is with Equiano as a spokesman for the African cause.

EQUIANO IN ENGLAND

Equiano finally settled in England in the 1770s. By the 1780s he had become deeply involved in the politics of the black people, championing their cause and fighting for the abolition of the slave trade. In his role as the black spokesman, he made contacts with such influential and sympathetic whites as Granville Sharp. It was Equiano, for example, who informed Sharp about the *Zong* murders. Sharp recorded on March 19, 1783, that "Gustavus Vassa, a negro, called on me, with an account of 130 negroes being thrown alive into the sea." That Equiano played the most important part in bringing the *Zong* murders to the public eye there can be no doubt. Sharp says that Equiano not only told him about the murders, but also pleaded with him to do something to bring the culprits to justice. As he says, he finally took the case to court "having been earnestly solicited and called upon by a poor negro for my assistance to avenge the blood of his slaughtered countrymen." Here then, we see an African actively involved in securing justice for his people. The fact that in the end, he did not succeed in getting the offenders convicted and punished is not the issue here. What is important is that Equiano acted in the *Zong* affair and, in conjunction with Sharp, General James Oglethorpe and other sympathizers, brought this shocking case before the court and the public.

By the late 1780s Equiano had become the recognized leader of the black community in Britain. . . . In 1785 he and other Africans addressed a letter to the Quakers, thanking them for their campaign against slavery and the slave trade. This action again shows Equiano's wide contacts with people and organizations sympathetic to the African cause. In 1786 Equiano's qualities of leadership were recognized by the British Government which appointed him His Majesty's Commissary for Stores for the Black Poor going to Sierra Leone. This appointment, however, was terminated in March 1787, before the expedition left Plymouth for Sierra

Leone. The fact that he was dismissed because of his outspoken defence of the black people against the high-handed actions of Joseph Irwin, the Agent, is particularly significant, for it shows his unwillingness to be an instrument of his own people's exploitation. He clearly took seriously his responsibilities as Commissary and as a black man. By protesting loudly and vigorously against Irwin and by openly accusing him of callousness and high-handedness in his dealings with the prospective settlers, he was giving notice that he was no Uncle Tom. He was prepared to risk challenging the establishment itself in order to obtain justice. . . .

EQUIANO'S NARRATIVE

In 1789 Equiano published his autobiography, *The Interesting Narrative of Olaudah Equiano or Gustavus Vassa, the African,* as a contribution to the anti-slavery campaign. The book proved popular, going, before 1800, into eight editions in Britain alone, as well as being translated into Dutch and German. Equiano himself travelled widely in England, Scotland and Ireland, selling his book and speaking against slavery.

The *Narrative* gives details of Equiano's travels as a slave and as a freeman, campaigning with Wolfe's army in Canada and Boscawen's fleet in the Mediterranean, as a merchant seaman in the West Indies and as a Surgeon's mate in the Phipps Expedition to the Arctic in 1772. However, it is much more than a catalogue of places and events, although these are interesting in themselves. At a deeper level the book shows Equiano's attitude to important issues of the day as they affected a black man and a slave. Take, as an example, his account of his impotence against force oppressing him. In the winter of 1762–63 he is re-sold and sent back into slavery. When he tells Captain Doran, his new master, that Captain Pascal could not have sold him, the reply which he gets is simple, but shattering:

> "Why," said he, "did not your master buy you?" I confessed he did. "But I have served him," said I, "many years, and he has taken all my wages and prize-money . . . besides this I have been baptized; and by the laws of the land no man has a right to sell me." And I added, that I had heard a lawyer and others . . . tell my master so. They both said that those people who told me so were not my friends."

When Equiano continues protesting against his slavery, "Captain Doran said I talked too much English; and if I did not behave myself well, and be quiet, he had a method on board to make me." Equiano is no fool. He knows that he is beaten: "I was too well convinced of his power over me to doubt what he said." Here then, we see, in no uncertain terms, the issue of authority or power as it was exercised over the black slaves. In these few lines is expressed the totality of that power. . . .

EQUIANO'S AMBIGUITY

Nevertheless, Equiano's behaviour was sometimes ambiguous. This is understandable when his alienation in the white world is considered. For example, throughout his travels he is always longing "to return to Old England." He longs to see "those pleasing scenes I left behind, where fair Liberty in bright array/Makes darkness bright, and e'en illumines day." Could it be that he has forgotten that the bright liberty which he talks about does not really shine for slaves in "Old England?" I do not think so. Despite these warm sentiments, Equiano was still an outsider, as all blacks were. If he had not been, he would not have campaigned as he did for the rights of black people. Also, when he finally settled in Old England he always designated himself as "the African." In other words, as an outsider in English society. Edwards puts it well when he says that Equiano, as an outsider "never ceases to be aware of himself (nor does the world let him) as a negro, a former slave, a member of a despised and maltreated race." We saw how, as Commissary for Stores, he came face to face with the sad reality of a black man in a white society. We saw how certain sections of the public in Old England attacked him in crude, racist tones. While there is no doubt about Equiano's love for England and its comparative freedom, there is equally no doubt about his awareness of the precarious position of a black man in it. This heightens the ambivalence in the book.

Ambivalence also exists elsewhere in the *Narrative*. For example, how should a slave react to a good master when, as in Equiano's case, he knows that slavery is in itself a bad thing? In the *Narrative*, as Edwards points out, the very whites who befriend Equiano are also involved in buying and selling his people. Because of this awareness, one is not sure what to think of the gratitude which Equiano expressed to Robert King for allowing him his freedom. It is possible to argue that King was a good man to allow him freedom at all, when other masters did not often do so. Yet it is no less true that it was freedom which Equiano bought by paying the full amount that King originally purchased him with. Such indeed is the high price, despite Farmer's telling King that "Gustavus has earned you more than a hundred a year, and will still save you money, as he will not leave you." What is clear is that black men were vulnerable to all the whims and caprices of the slave owner. The ambivalence in Equiano is just an indication of that insecurity and confusion.

There is even greater ambiguity when Captain Farmer dies and Equiano takes charge of the ship. Farmer's death means the loss of one of Equiano's best benefactors, but it also gives him the opportunity to display his skill as a navigator and his qualities as a leader. He himself puts it thus:

> I now obtained a new appelation and was called Captain. This elated me not a little and it was flattering to my vanity to be thus styled by as high a title as any man in this place possessed.

And in another episode, as a result of the incompetence of one of his Captains, Equiano takes charge of the ship, rather ironic for a former slave. And there are indications in the text that Equiano is not unaware of the irony.

As a black man in a white world and as a slave or ex-slave, Equiano had to keep adapting to new and sometimes contrary experiences. It was these experiences, perspectives of, and insights into white society which prepared him well for the leadership of the black community. As [historian James] Walvin says, "In his great range of occupations, as slave, sailor, domestic, commissary, princely African and black Englishman and friend to the new 'popular' London radicals, Equiano was able to speak with greater authority and assurance than [Ignatius] Sancho, [another former slave turned antislavery activist prominent in England] whose life had been, in black terms, relatively sheltered."

This was a fact recognized by the Society for the Abolition of the Slave Trade. In a manuscript letter of 1792, Equiano wrote about his role in the campaign against slavery and the slave trade: "I trust that my going about has been of much use in the Cause of the accu(r)sed Slave Trade—a Gentleman of the Committee the Rev. Dr. Baker has said that I am more use to the Cause than half the people in the Country—I wish to God I could be so."

His writings and activities clearly suggest that abolition was the most important cause of his life in England. He did everything he could to further the black cause.

Life After Freedom: Fulfilling the American Dream

Sidonie Smith

The Civil War and the Thirteenth Amendment to the
U.S. Constitution, enacted in 1865, ended American
slavery. Nonetheless, former slaves continued to
publish their life stories. The escape to freedom,
however, was not at the heart of these postbellum
slave narratives; the narrator instead focused on his
or her life after emancipation. For the former slave
after the Civil War, freedom meant entering the
mainstream of American life by achieving economic
success. Sidonie Smith examines the career of
Booker T. Washington, author of *Up from Slavery* in
this chapter from *Where I'm Bound: Patterns of Slavery and Freedom in Black American Autobiography*.
Smith sees Washington as the African American embodiment of the Horatio Alger hero, the man of mod-
est birth who achieves success in American society
through honesty and hard work. Although Washington strongly resembles other slave narrators, he
more closely resembles Benjamin Franklin in his
quest for fame and fortune.

Booker T. Washington was probably the first well-known
black Horatio Alger. "By the beginning of the new century,
Washington," explains John Hope Franklin in an introduction to one edition of the autobiography,

> was one of the most powerful men in the United States. Great
> philanthropists and industrialists such as Andrew Carnegie
> and John D. Rockefeller listened to him courteously and were
> influenced by his advice. Presidents such as Theodore Roo-
> sevelt and William Howard Taft depended on him for sugges-
> tions regarding the resolution of problems involving race.

Excerpted from Sidonie Smith, *Where I'm Bound: Patterns of Slavery and Freedom in
Black American Autobiography*. Copyright © 1974 Sidonie Smith. Reprinted with permission from Greenwood Publishing Group, Inc., Westport, CT.

Southern whites in high places knew that a good word in their behalf by Washington would open doors previously closed to them.

After achieving such stature and power in American society, Washington was urged by others to write his autobiography. The popularity of *Up from Slavery,* which became a best-seller soon after publication, indicated how inspiring his rise to fame had been. His life was an embodiment of the possibility of self-improvement, made powerful and tangible by his preference for objective reality. "I have great faith in the power and influence of facts," writes Washington early in the work.

I have found, too, that it is the visible, the tangible, that goes a long ways in softening prejudice. The actual sight of a first-class house that a Negro has built is ten times more potent than pages of discussion about a house that he ought to build, or perhaps could build.

His exemplary life is just such a tangible "house," and the narrative of his rise to fame is designed to relate the material facts of its evolutionary construction within society.

WASHINGTON'S HUMBLE BEGINNINGS

A sense of mystery pervades the first paragraph of the auto-biography. Washington does not know the exact place or date of his birth; he "suspects [he] must have been born somewhere and at some time." To this initial sense of mystery, the second paragraph adds the quality of life—desolate poverty—and the third paragraph his anonymous ancestry. Although Washington knew his mother's name, he admits: "Of my father I knew even less than of my mother. I do not even know his name." The prominent leader enters the drama of life as a semi-orphan, spawned mysteriously from nowhere, secured by no ancestral roots, environed by humble conditions. This beginning sharpens the contrast with his social position fifty years later at the time of writing and underscores the fact that whatever he achieved he achieved single-handedly.

Soon after emancipation, Washington, as did other former slaves, named himself. The child's choice of name is particularly revealing: by naming himself "Washington"—a name associated with patriotism, American democracy, social prominence, and leadership—Booker, prompted by a belief in the society into which he was born and a need to be a part of and a leader in that society, creates an ideal identity which embodies his personal vision of himself. Naming becomes a prophetic, baptismal ritual.

The next rite of passage of Washington's journey is the "effort to fit [himself] to accomplish the most good in the world."

Booker T. Washington

The early part of his narrative, therefore, centers on his struggle to secure an education, first at Kanawha Valley school and then at Hampton Institute, which, interestingly enough, he describes as "the promised land." Thereafter, the autobiography becomes the narrative of Washington's work, an open-ended exposition of his public efforts to better the conditions of his race, especially through the founding and growth of Tuskegee Institute. He focuses his narrative, as he did his life, on the material obstacles he had to overcome—money to finance new buildings, furniture, clothing for the students, and so on and on. In the process of surmounting these obstacles, Washington assumes the position of leadership which fulfills the destiny inherent in the name.

WASHINGTON AND FRANKLIN

The many parallels between Washington's success story and that of Benjamin Franklin are striking and suggest the degree to which Washington is simply giving us the black version of a well-known formula. Both men, growing restless at an early age because their overwhelming need for self-improvement remains unsatisfied, journey to a distant city that offers them an opportunity to fulfill that need. Both describe their entry into the city similarly, stressing, by implication, the disparity between their early status and their prominence at the moment of writing. Here is Franklin's entrance into Philadelphia in 1723:

> I have been the more particular in this description of my journey, and shall be so of my first entry into that city, that you

may in your mind compare such unlikely beginnings with the figure I have since made there. I was in my working dress, my best clothes being to come round by sea. I was dirty from my journey; my pockets were stuffed out with shirts and stockings; I knew no soul, nor where to look for lodging. Fatigued with walking, rowing, and want of rest, I was very hungry, and my whole stock of cash consisted of a Dutch dollar and about a shilling in copper coin, which I gave to the boatmen for my passage. At first they refused it on account of my having rowed; but I insisted on their taking it. A man is sometimes more generous when he has little money than when he has plenty, perhaps through fear of being thought to have but little. I walked towards the top of the street, gazing about till near Market Street, where I met a boy with bread. I have often made a meal of dry bread, and inquiring where he had bought it, I went immediately to the baker's he directed me to. I asked for bisket, meaning such as we had in Boston; but that sort, it seems, was not made in Philadelphia. I then asked for a three penny loaf and was told they had none such. Not knowing the different prices nor the names of the different sorts of bread, I told him to give me three pennyworth of any sort. He gave me accordingly three great puffy rolls. I was surprised at the quantity but took it, and having no room in my pockets, walked off with a roll under each arm and eating the other. Thus I went up Market Street as far as Fourth Street, passing by the door of Mr. Read, my future wife's father; when she, standing at the door, saw me, and thought I made—as I certainly did—a most awkward, ridiculous appearance. Then I turned and went down Chestnut Street and part of Walnut Street, eating my roll all the way, and coming round, found myself again at Market Street wharf near the boat I came in, to which I went for a draught of the river water, and being filled with one of my rolls, gave the other two to a woman and her child that came down the river in the boat with us and were waiting to go farther.

Washington's description of his entry into Richmond in 1872 echoes Franklin's self-portraiture and his chronology of concerns:

By walking, begging rides both in wagons and in the cars, in some way, after a number of days, I reached the city of Richmond, Virginia, about eighty-two miles from Hampton. When I reached there, tired, hungry, and dirty, it was late in the night. I had never been in a large city, and this rather added to my misery. When I reached Richmond, I was completely out of money. I had not it single acquaintance in the place, and, being unused to city ways, I did not know where to go. I applied at several places for lodging, but they all wanted money, and that was what I did not have. Knowing nothing else better to do, I walked the streets. In doing this I passed by many foodstands where fried chicken and half-moon apple pies were piled high and made to present a most tempting appearance. At that time it seemed to me that I would have promised all that I expected to possess in the future to have gotten hold of one of those chicken legs or one of those pies. But I could not get either of these, nor anything else to eat.

I must have walked the streets till after midnight. At last I became so exhausted that I could walk no longer. I was tired, I was hungry, I was everything but discouraged. Just about the time when I reached extreme physical exhaustion, I came upon a portion of a street where the board sidewalk was considerably elevated. I waited for a few minutes, till I was sure that no passers-by could see me, and then crept under the sidewalk and lay for the night upon the ground, with my satchel of clothing for a pillow.

Both men go on to describe their gradual rise to social prominence and focus on their endeavors in behalf of others, Franklin on his social projects for Philadelphia and the nation, Washington with his program for Negro betterment.

AN AFRICAN AMERICAN HORATIO ALGER

Even this brief summary of parallels is sufficient to rearticulate the fundamental ethos behind the Horatio Alger myth, whether black or white. This hero is an economic materialist, an industrious, self-made businessman who views the world as material to be conquered in his rise to success. He is a public man, a man of action whose sense of identity and self-fulfillment derive from his social usefulness. He is a virtuous man who upholds middle-class mores and morals. The ethos of Washington's life journey mirrors the predominant ethos of the time; therein lies its power and its influence. *Up from Slavery* is a businessman's autobiography, which is the reason why it met such success in the United States and abroad at a time when business was becoming big business and when the Horatio Alger myth itself was extremely popular, embodied as it was in current fiction and such autobiographies as that of Andrew Carnegie. But it met with success primarily because Washington responded as a businessman would to the social climate of the late nineteenth century—a time when the black American was being systematically deprived of political and civil rights—by adopting a pragmatic stance that mirrored the white attitudinal climate. The exuberant hope of post-war Reconstruction had been shattered; a more realistic hope, deriving from

a program of self-help, of assimilation into and accommo-
dation with the dominant culture, replaced it.

The situations that Washington and Franklin describe
above, however, are only almost identical, and the differences that lie in the "almost" embody the essential disparity
between the white and black versions of the journey of the
Horatio Alger hero. Franklin had some money and his good
clothes were being sent to him; Washington had neither.
Franklin could give food away; Washington could buy none
at all. Franklin did not worry about lodging; Washington
could find none but the space beneath the boardwalk. The
obstacles along the black Horatio Alger's way, whether social, economic, or political, radically limit the fluidity of his
movement in American society. They are literally antagonis-
tic and potentially destructive. Nevertheless, through a strict
moral rectitude, Washington does manage to transform even
this radical difference from a liability into an asset:

> With few exceptions, the Negro youth must work harder and
> must perform his task even better than a white youth in or-
> der to secure recognition. But out of the hard and unusual
> struggle which he is compelled to pass, he gets a strength, a
> confidence, that one misses whose pathway is comparatively
> smooth by reason of birth and race.

In the end, Washington's optimism and faith in the system are reaffirmed in his appropriation of an autobiographical form that embodies the traditional American
myth of social success. *Up from Slavery*, articulated in the
formal language of the dominant culture, serves as a vehicle for discussing a philosophy acceptable to the dominant
culture and for dramatizing, to both blacks and whites, the
success of that philosophy.

CHAPTER 4

Gender Issues in the Slave Narrative

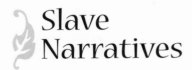

Slave
Narratives

The Development of Women's Slave Narratives

Henry Louis Gates Jr.

Henry Louis Gates Jr., chair of the Department of Afro-American Studies at Harvard University, is the author of several seminal critical works on African American literature, including *Figures in Black* and *The Signifying Monkey*. He has edited *The Norton Anthology of African American Literature*, *The Classic Slave Narratives*, and *The Civitas Anthology of African American Slave Narratives*. In this excerpt from his introduction to *The Classic Slave Narratives*, Gates discusses the development of women's slave narratives, which "'broke the silence' of the black woman slave." Gates's discussion focuses on two of the most important women's slave narratives of the mid-nineteenth century, *The History of Mary Prince* and Harriet Jacobs's *Incidents in the Life of a Slave Girl*.

Mary Prince, born a slave at Brackish-Pond in Bermuda, enjoys the distinction of being the first woman to publish a slave narrative. This short narrative of twenty-three pages appeared in two editions at London in 1831. Although it is noteworthy for being the first woman's story, it is even more noteworthy because it altered fundamentally the very genre of the slave narratives.

MARY PRINCE'S NARRATIVE

Though Prince's story begins in the classic "I was born" mode common to all slave narratives, she quickly alerts her readers to the fact that hers is a tale that has not been told before, the very tale of the female slave who heretofore had been spoken for but who had not yet spoken *for herself.* Whereas both [Olaudah] Equiano and [Frederick] Douglass were concerned with depicting the cruelties of slavery by providing a few vivid scenes of sadism and sexual abuse practiced by white masters and mistresses against black women, Prince's account makes her readers acutely aware that the sexual brutalization of the black woman slave— along with the enforced severance of a mother's natural relation to her children and lover of her choice—defined more than any other aspect of slavery the daily price of her bondage. Whereas black women are objects of narration in the tales written by black men, Prince's slim yet compelling story celebrates their self-transformation into subjects, subjects as defined by those who have gained a voice.

Prince is a convincing narrator, one who combines a fine sense of metaphor with the compulsion to testify and indict her oppressors: "Slavery hardens white people's hearts toward the blacks; and many of them were not slow to make their remarks upon us aloud, without regard to our grief— though their light words fell like cayenne on the fresh wounds of our hearts." Prince also reveals that sadism was as commonly practiced by white women as by white men; her own mistress "caused me to know the exact difference between the smart of the rope, the cart-whip, and the cow-skin, when applied to my naked body by her own cruel hand. . . . To strip me naked—to hang me up by the wrists and lay my flesh open with the cow-skin, was an ordinary punishment for even a slight offense." Her master beat her in the same way, but also forced her "to wash him in a tub of water" after he had "stripped himself quite naked." This, she confesses, was "worse to me than all the licks." Slavery brutalized men and women, mistress and master, the enslaved and the free.

Prince's narrative is also central to the development of the slave narrative because she repeatedly comments upon the differences between popular white myths or impressions about the feelings of slaves, and the actual feelings of the slaves themselves: "Oh the Bucka [white] people who keep slaves think that black people are like cattle, without natural affection. But my heart tells me it is otherwise." Near the conclusion of her narrative, Prince makes an even bolder claim: "All slaves want to be free—to be free is very sweet. . . . I have been a slave myself—I know what slaves feel—I can tell by myself what other slaves feel, and by what they have told me. The man that says slaves be quite happy in slavery—

that they don't want to be free—that man is either ignorant or a lying person." As William Andrews concludes about Prince's statement:

> In this remark a black female slave declares herself to be a more reliable authority on slavery than any white man and fully capable of speaking for all her fellow slaves, both male and female, against any white man. The implication of this declaration should not be underestimated, since it provides the first claim in the Afro-American autobiographical tradition for the black woman as singularly authorized to represent all black people, regardless of gender, in Western discourse about "what slaves feel" about the morality of slavery.

HARRIET JACOBS'S NARRATIVE

If Prince's narrative "broke the silence" of the black woman slave, Harriet Jacobs's *Incidents in the Life of a Slave Girl* brought this category of slave narratives to its summit. As William Andrews says, Jacobs's *Incidents* is "the major black woman's autobiography of the mid-nineteenth century." *Incidents* is also one of the major autobiographies in the Afro-American tradition.

Despite its great distinction as a remarkably well-written narrative and as a testament to the human will to survive, Jacobs's narrative has only recently been authenticated as "written by herself," as her subtitle claims. Published under the pseudonym of "Linda Brent," "edited" by the well-known anti-slavery writer, Lydia Maria Child, and constructed around an astonishing plot (in which the heroine remains concealed from her master for seven years in a garret in her grandmother's home), Jacobs's narrative was long thought to be either a novel assuming the shape of a slave narrative—as was Mattie Griffiths's *Autobiography of a Female Slave* (1857) or Richard Hildreth's *The Slave; or, Memoirs of Archy Moore* (1836)—or else a ghost-written autobiography that strained credibility. The classic statement of the fraudulence of Jacobs's work is that written by John W. Blassingame in *The Slave Community* (1972):

> In spite of Lydia Maria Child's insistence that she had only revised the manuscript of Harriet Jacobs "mainly for purpose of condensation and orderly arrangement," the work is not credible. In the first place, *Incidents in the Life of a Slave Girl* (1861), is too orderly; too many of the major characters meet providentially after years of separation. Then, too, the story is too melodramatic: miscegenation and cruelty, outraged virtue, unrequited love, and planter licentiousness appear on practi-

cally every page. The virtuous Harriet sympathizes with her wretched mistress who has to look on all of the mulattoes fathered by her husband, she refuses to bow to the lascivious demands of her master, bears two children for another white man, and then runs away and hides in a garret in her grandmother's cabin for seven years until she is able to escape to New York. In the meantime, her white lover has acknowledged his paternity of her children, purchased their freedom, and been elected to Congress. In the end, all live happily ever after.

Despite the fact that an 1861 reviewer writing in *The Anti-Slavery Advocate* claims an extended acquaintance with the author and vouches with great confidence for the authenticity of her tale, it was not until 1981 that a scholar, Jean Fagan Yellin, demonstrated conclusively that Jacobs indeed wrote the narrative of her bondage and freedom. Few instances of scholarly inquiry have been more important to Afro-American studies than has Yellin's.

Jacobs's narrative is a bold and gripping fusion of two major literary forms: she borrowed from the popular sentimental novel on one hand, and the slave narrative genre on the other. Jacobs's tale gains its importance from the fact that she charts, in great and painful detail, the sexual exploitation that daily haunted her life—and the lives of every other black female slave. In the character of the unrelentingly evil Dr. Flint, and in the hard choices that his vulgar pursuit forces Jacobs to make, Jacobs graphically renders the sexual aspect of economic exploitation in a manner unimaginable before. Whereas the black male slave narrators' accounts of sexual brutality remain suggestive, if gruesome, Jacobs's—enlarging upon the precedent created by Mary Prince—charts vivid detail by vivid detail precisely how the shape of her life and the choices she makes are defined by her reduction to a sexual object, an object to be raped, bred, or abused. To escape the repulsive advances of Dr. Flint, she becomes the lover of a white man called Sands, to whom she bears two children, whom Sands promises to free. Banished by an outraged Flint to another plantation and taunted by the threat of the permanent loss of the possibility of freedom for her children, Jacobs escapes, hides in a garret in her grandmother's home (three feet high, nine feet long, and seven feet wide) for seven years. Jacobs even writes letters in her garret, then has these mailed to Flint from Boston and New York, cleverly deceiving him. Sands does purchase and liberate his children, and Jacobs and the children eventually escape to the North, where more subtle modes of oppression await.

Jacobs revises the received structure of the genre as practiced by its two great exemplars, Equiano and Douglass, by framing her entire story with descriptions of the inherent strength, dignity, and nobility of her family, and especially that of her maternal grandmother, in whom she "had a great treasure," as she informs her readers in her very first paragraph. In so doing, she engages in one of the earliest examples of literary female bonding in the black tradition. And she also appeals directly to a female readership, including whites, by selecting as one of her epigraphs Isaiah 22:9: "Rise up! ye women that are at ease! Hear my voice, ye careless daughters!" This act, what feminists today would call "gendering," represents a major break from the male tradition she inherited.

In the final paragraph of the narrative, Jacobs reflects upon the pains of her enslavement, finding comfort only in one set of memories:

> It has been painful to me, in many ways, to recall the dreary years I passed in bondage. I would gladly forget them if I could. Yet the retrospection is not altogether without solace; for with those gloomy recollections come tender memories of my good old grandmother, like light, fleecy clouds floating over a dark and troubled sea.

In this way, Jacobs stresses not only the central importance of her grandmother in her own life, but also the crucial centrality of female bonding in the life of the slave woman. This declaration, along with the fact that Jacobs here has remodeled the forms of the black slave narrative and the white female sentimental novel to create a new literary form—a narrative at once black and female—underscores the major importance of *Incidents in the Life of a Slave Girl* to the Afro-American literary tradition.

Defining the Slave Narrative in Female Terms

Joanne M. Braxton

Joanne M. Braxton, a feminist poet and literary scholar, argues for a redefinition of the slave narrative. According to Braxton, the criticism concerning the slave narrative has focused on narratives written by men, such as those authored by Olaudah Equiano and Frederick Douglass, and has relegated narratives written by women to positions of secondary importance. Braxton's essay centers on Harriet Jacobs's *Incidents in the Life of a Slave Girl* and argues that Jacobs's text, which focuses on the sexual abuse of slave women and their difficulties in retaining and raising their children, speaks for the lives of many African American women held in bondage. Braxton calls for a "more balanced view" of the slave narrative genre, one that includes those written by women.

In general, the purpose of the slave narrative genre is to decry the cruelty and brutality of slavery and to bring about its abolition. In addition, the genre has been defined as possessing certain other characteristics, including a narrator who speaks in a coherent, first person voice, with a range and scope of knowledge like that of an unlettered slave and a narrative movement which progresses from South to North, and culminates in an escape from slavery to a freedom which is both an inner and outer liberation. The prevalent themes of the genre include the deprivation of food, clothing, and shelter, the desire for instruction (frequently for religious instruction, which is thwarted), physical brutality, the corruption of families (usually white), the separation of families (usually black), the exploitation of slave workers and, in some narratives, especially those written by

Excerpted from Joanne M. Braxton, "Harriet Jacobs' *Incidents in the Life of a Slave Girl:* The Redefinition of the Slave Narrative Genre," *Massachusetts Review,* vol. 27, pp. 379–87, 1986. Copyright © 1986 The Massachusetts Review, Inc. Reprinted with permission from *The Massachusetts Review.*

women, abuse of the sexuality and reproductive powers of the slave woman.

THE MALE BIAS

The resistance to a gynocritical or gynocentric approach to the slave narrative genre has been dominated by male bias, by linear logic, and by either/or thinking. We have been paralyzed by issues of primacy, and authorship, and by criteria of unity, coherence, completion, and length. Academic systems, which do not value scholarship of black women or reward it, have told us that we are not first, not central, not major, not authentic. The suggestion has been that neither the lives of black women nor the study of our narratives and autobiographies have been legitimate.

I want to supplement the either/or thinking that has limited the consideration of evidence surrounding the narratives of women, and the inclusion of such works in the slave narrative genre. Instead of asking "Is it first? Is it major? Is it central? Does it conform to established criteria?" this study asks, "How would the inclusion of works by women change the shape of the genre?"

To begin with, the inclusion of works by women would push the origin of the slave narrative genre back by two years, and root it more firmly in American soil, for the genre begins, not with *The Interesting Narrative of Olaudah Equiano, or Gustavus Vassa, the African*, published in London in 1789, but with the narrative of a slave woman entitled "Belinda, or the Cruelty of Men Whose Faces Were Like the Moon," published in the United States in 1787, a narrative of a few pages which would be considered too short by conventional standards.

Traditionally, the 1845 *Narrative of the Life of Frederick Douglass, An American Slave, Written by Himself*, has been viewed as the central text in the genre, and based on this narrative, critic Robert Stepto has defined the primary Afro-American archetype as that of the articulate hero who discovers the "bonds among freedom, literacy, and struggle." Once again, the narrative experience of the articulate and rationally enlightened female slave has not been part of the definition. Stepto, in his otherwise brilliant work on the *Narrative of the Life of Frederick Douglass, An American Slave, Written by Himself* (1845), makes no attempt to define a corresponding female archetype; I propose that we consider as a counterpart to the articulate hero the archetype of the outraged mother. She appears repeatedly in Afro-American history and literary tradition, and she is fully represented in Harriet "Linda Brent" Jacobs' *Incidents in the Life of a Slave Girl: Written by Herself* (1861).

IGNORING FEMALE NARRATIVES

Although Thayer and Eldridge published *Incidents in the Life of a Slave Girl* in Boston in 1861, not until 1981 did Jean F. Yellin publish evidence establishing Jacobs' historical identity and the authorship of her narrative. Marion Starling, a black woman, had argued for the authenticity of the Jacobs narrative as early as 1947, but male critics like Sterling Brown and Arna Bontemps contested that authorship. The issue was complicated by the fact that Lydia Maria Child had edited the Jacobs narrative, which was published under the pseudonym, Linda Brent.

In general, the kinds of questions asked about the text prohibited scholars from seeing *Incidents* as part of the slave narrative genre and prevented them from looking for historical evidence to establish Jacobs' authorship. Yellin found such evidence readily available in the form of letters from Jacobs to Lydia Maria Child, from Jacobs to her confidante, Rochester Quaker Amy Post, and also in letters from Lydia Maria Child to John Greenleaf Whittier and William Lloyd Garrison, as well as the apprentice pieces Jacobs published in the New York *Tribune.*

Another piece of external evidence overlooked by many scholars is a May 1, 1861 review of *Incidents* which appeared in the London *Anti-Slavery Advocate* written by a reviewer who had knowledge of the manuscript in both the original and published versions and who also had talked with the author. This *Anti-Slavery Advocate* review contains a wonderful description of Jacobs and her text:

> We have read this book with no ordinary interest, for we are acquainted with the writer; and have heard many of the incidents from her own lips, and have great confidence in her truthfulness and integrity. Between two and three years ago, a coloured woman, about as dark as a southern Spaniard or a Portuguese, aged about five-and-forty, with a kind and pleasing expression of countenance, called on us, bearing an introductory letter from one of the most honoured friends of the anti-slavery cause in the United States. This letter requested our friendly offices on behalf of Linda, who was desirous of publishing her narrative in England. It happened that the friends at whose house we were then staying were so

much interested by this dusky stranger's conversation and demeanour, that they induced her to become their guest for some weeks. Thus we had an excellent opportunity of becoming acquainted with one of the greatest heroines we have ever met with. Her manners were marked by refinement and sensibility, and by an utter absence of pretense or affectation; and we were deeply touched by the circumstances of her early life which she then communicated, and which exactly coincide with those of the volume now before us.

This kind of evidence establishes both the authenticity and primacy many critics have denied *Incidents in the Life of a Slave Girl*. Had these scholars asked the same questions of *Incidents* they asked of male narratives, had they looked for external evidence and examined it carefully, they would have come to the conclusion that Linda Brent wrote this narrative herself.

But as I have suggested, questions about unity, length, primacy and authorship are not the most important ones we can ask of such a narrative. We can more profitably ask how reading the work modifies an understanding of the slave narrative genre. However, the fact remains that the established criteria used to define the slave narrative genre have systematically excluded women; this paper calls those criteria into question.

JACOBS SPEAKS FOR WOMEN

When viewed from a gynocritical or gynocentric perspective, *Incidents* arrives at the very heart and root of Afra-American autobiographical writing. Although other works appear earlier, this full-length work by an Afra-American writing about her experiences as a slave woman is indeed rare. Yet despite its rarity, *Incidents* speaks for many lives; it is in many respects a representative document.

Incidents is descended both from the autobiographical tradition of the heroic male slaves and a line of American women's writings that attacks racial oppression and sexual exploitation. It combines the narrative pattern of the slave narrative genre with the conventional literary forms and stylistic devices of the 19th century domestic novel in an attempt to transform the so-called "cult of true womanhood" and to persuade the women of the North to take a public stand against slavery, the most political issue of the day. The twin themes of abolition and feminism are interwoven in Jacobs' text.

Like Harriet Beecher Stowe's hybrid, *Uncle Tom's Cabin*,

Incidents focuses on the power relationships of masters and slaves and the ways in which (slave) women learn to manage the invasive sexuality of (white) men. Unlike Stowe, who demonstrates her anxiety about the authorship of *Uncle Tom's Cabin* by saying that God wrote it, the author of *Incidents* claims responsibility for every word, and yet she publishes under the pseudonym "Linda Brent."

THE EXPLOITATION OF FEMALE SLAVES

In this excerpt from Incidents in the Life of a Slave Girl, *Harriet Jacobs records the process by which female slaves were sexually exploited by their male masters.*

No pen can give adequate description of the all-pervading corruption produced by slavery. The slave girl is reared in an atmosphere of licentiousness and fear. The lash and the foul talk of her master and his sons are her teachers. When she is fourteen or fifteen, her owner, or his sons, or the overseer, or perhaps all of them, begin to bribe her with presents. If these fail to accomplish their purpose, she is whipped or starved into submission to their will. She may have had religious principles inculcated by some pious mother or grandmother, or some good mistress; she may have a lover, whose good opinion and peace of mind are dear to her heart; or the profligate men who have power over her may be exceedingly odious to her. But resistance is hopeless.

Harriet Jacobs, *Incidents in the Life of a Slave Girl,* 1861.

Although I had read the critical literature on women's autobiographies, it was *Incidents* that taught me that the silences and gaps in the narrative of women's lives are sometimes more significant than the filled spaces. "Linda Brent" obscures the names of persons and places mentioned in the text, and although she denies any need for secrecy on her own part, she writes that she deemed it "kind and considerate toward others to pursue this course." Thus she speaks as a disguised woman, whose identity remains partly obscured. A virtual "madwoman in the attic," Linda leads a veiled and unconventional life. Her dilemma is that of life under slavery as a beautiful, desirable female slave, object of desire as well as profit.

Linda adheres to a system of black and female cultural values that motivate her actions and inform the structure of this text. First of all, the author's stated purpose is to "arouse the woman of the North to a realizing sense of the condition of two millions of women at the South." If the white women of the North know the true conditions of the slave women of the South, then they cannot fail to answer Jacobs' call to moral action.

In order to balance our understanding of the slave narrative genre, we need first to read those narratives written by women (and to read them closely), and secondly to expand the range of terms used in writing about those narratives. An analysis of the imagery, thematic content, uses of language, and patterns of narrative movement in *Incidents in the Life of A Slave Girl* moves us closer to a characterization of the behavior of the outraged mother and to a more balanced understanding of the slave narrative genre.

RESISTING OPPRESSION

As one who is small and relatively powerless in the face of her oppression, the outraged mother makes use of wit and intelligence to overwhelm and defeat a more powerful foe. In her aspect as trickster, "Linda" employs defensive verbal postures as well as various forms of disguise and concealment to outwit and escape Dr. Flint, the archetypal patriarchal rapist slavemaster:

1. She must conceal her quest for literacy and her ability to read in order to prevent the master from slipping her foul notes in an attempt to seduce her.

2. She must conceal her love for a free black man she eventually sends away for his own good, as well as the identity of the white man who becomes the father of her children and who eventually betrays her.

3. She conceals her pregnancy from everyone.

4. She must conceal her plans to run away, working hard and attempting to appear contented during the time she formulates these plans.

5. When Linda "runs away," she is disguised as a man and taken to the Snaky Swamp, a location she finds more hospitable than landed slave culture.

6. She is then concealed in the home of a neighboring white woman (a slaveholder sympathetic to her plight), and, finally, in a crawl space in her grandmother's house for seven years.

7. While concealed in her grandmother's house, Linda de-

ceives the master by writing letters a friend mails from New York. When Flint takes off to New York to look for the fugitive, she is practically in his own back yard.

8. Linda is taken to the North in disguise, and even after she arrives there, she must conceal her identity with a veil, which she only removes when her freedom is purchased by a group of Northern white women. Through quick-thinking, the use of sass and invective, and a series of deceptions, Linda finally realizes freedom for herself and her children.

SASS AS A WEAPON

"Sass" is a word of West African derivation associated with the female aspect of the trickster figure. The OED attributes the origin of "sass" to the "sassy tree," the powerfully poisonous Erythophloeum quineense (Cynometra Manni). A decoction of the bark of this tree was used in West Africa as an ordeal poison in the trial of accused witches, women spoken of as being wives of Exu, the trickster god. According to the 1893 *Autobiography* of Mrs. Amanda Smith,

> I don't know as any one has ever found what the composition of this sassy wood really is; but I am told it is a mixture of certain barks. There is a tree there which grows very tall, called the sassy wood tree, but there is something mixed with this which is very difficult to find out, and the natives do not tell what it is. They say that it is one of their medicines that they use to carry out their law for punishing witches; so you cannot find out what it is.

"The accused had *two gallons* to drink. If she throws it up, she has gained her case," Mrs. Smith wrote. So "sass" can kill.

Webster's Third International Dictionary defines "sass" as talking impudently or disrespectfully to an elder or a superior, or as talking back. Throughout the text, Linda uses "sass" as a weapon of self-defense whenever she is under sexual attack by the master; she returns a portion of the poison he has offered her. In one instance Dr. Flint demands: "Do you know that I have a right to do as I like with you,—that I can kill you, if I please?" Negotiating for respect, Linda replies: "You have tried to kill me, and I wish you had; but you have no right to do as you like with me." "Sass" is an effective tool that allows "Linda" to preserve her self-esteem and to increase the psychological distance between herself and the master. She uses "sass" the way Frederick Douglass uses his fists and his feet, as a means of expressing her resistance.

It is a distinctive feature of the outraged mother that she sacrifices opportunities to escape without her children; Linda is motivated by an overwhelming concern for them, a concern not apparent in the narratives of the questing male slaves. This concern is shown in chapter titles like "A New Tie to Life," "Another Link to Life," "The Children Sold," "New Destination for the Children," and "The Meeting of Mother and Daughter."

The outraged mother resists her situation not so much on behalf of herself as on behalf of her children. She is part of a continuum; she links the dead, the living, and the unborn. "I knew the doom that awaited my fair baby in slavery, and I determined to save her from it, or perish in the attempt. I went to make this vow at the graves of my poor parents, in the burying ground of the slaves." In the case of Jacobs' narrative, the sense of the continuum of *women's* oppression is also clear.

It is the prospect of her daughter's life under slavery that finally nerves Jacobs to run away. "When they told me my new-born babe was a girl, my heart was heavier than it had ever been before. Slavery is a terrible thing for men; but it is far more terrible for women," Jacobs wrote. "Superadded to the burden common to all, *they* have wrongs, and sufferings and mortifications peculiarly their own."

Another important difference between this narrative and those of the heroic male slaves is that Linda celebrates the cooperation and collaboration of all the people, black and white, slave and free, who make her freedom possible. She celebrates her liberation and her children's as the fruit of a collective, not individual effort.

A More Balanced View of the Genre

The inclusion of *Incidents in the Life of a Slave Girl, Written by Herself* in the slave narrative genre and the autobiographical tradition of black Americans, permits a more balanced view of that genre and that tradition, presenting fresh themes, images, and uses of language. *Incidents* occupies a position as central to that tradition as the 1845 *Narrative of Frederick Douglass.* Only in this perspective does the outraged mother emerge as the archetypal counterpart of the articulate hero.

Further study of all such texts and testimonies by women will allow us to fill out an understanding of that experience and culture which I have designated as Afra-American, and help us correct and expand existing analyses based too exclusively on male models of experience and writing. The study of black women's writing helps us to transform definitions of genre, of archetype, of narrative traditions, and of the African-American experience itself.

The Exploitation of Female Slaves by Their White Mistresses

Minrose C. Gwin

In this essay, literary critic Minrose C. Gwin, the author of Black and White Women of the Old South: The Peculiar Sisterhood in American Literature, *discusses the relationship between white mistresses and their female African American slaves, as that relationship is depicted in slave narratives authored by women. According to Gwin, white mistresses exerted an abusive power over the slave women who served them; this relationship is made further problematic by the jealousy that white mistresses have for their female slaves, some of whom have sexual relationships with the husbands of the mistresses. Gwin's essay focuses on two slave narratives written by women, Harriet Jacobs's* Incidents in the Life of a Slave Girl *and Elizabeth Keckley's* Behind the Scenes: Thirty Years a Slave and Four Years in the White House.

In the mistress-slave relationship the white woman exerted ultimate power, and that power could transform sexual jealousy into intense cruelty. The abolitionists' slogan that complete power corrupts is nowhere more apparent than in the relationships between these southern women, whose common bonds of suffering and dehumanization might have bound them in mutual compassion. Stephen Butterfield points out that black autobiography is often a "mirror of white deeds"; and it is in the slave narratives, not in the white women's journals and reminiscences, that the jealous mistress springs to life in all of her fury and perversity. Particularly in two women's narratives of the 1860s, the jealous mistress becomes a symbol of the narrators' past powerlessness and of the terror and degradation perpetrated under the

Excerpted from Minrose C. Gwin, "Green-Eyed Monsters of the Slavocracy: Jealous Mistresses in Two Slave Narratives," in *Conjuring: Black Women, Fiction, and Literary Tradition*, edited by Marjorie Pryse and Hortense J. Spillers. Copyright © 1985 Indiana University Press. Reprinted with permission from Indiana University Press.

South's "peculiar institution." Harriet Jacobs's *Incidents in the Life of a Slave Girl* (1861) and Elizabeth Keckley's *Behind the Scenes: Thirty Years a Slave and Four Years in the White House* (1868), perhaps the two best-known women's book-length slave narratives of the nineteenth century, depict former mistresses as cruel, jealous, vindictive women. Yet, in remaking their own lives in language, both Jacobs and Keckley exert upon these white women the control that they as mistresses formerly exerted upon them as slaves. In this sense these narratives become avenues of self-determination and of emotional freedom from the specter of slavery. As Jacobs and Keckley reshape their lives as slaves and reenact the cruelties of their jealous mistresses, they remake and strengthen themselves as ontological beings in a free world where cross-racial female bonds are possible.

Victims of the Institution

The two black women write of their resentments against their mistresses, but not with as much total condemnation as a contemporary reader might expect. As Frances Foster points out, writers of the slave narratives, both men and women, were writing to a white audience. In the antebellum and Civil War periods, the slave narratives were designed first of all to convince a white northern audience that slavery was wrong—not just for the slave but for everyone. Wronged mistresses were depicted as cruel and vindictive, but they were also construed as victims themselves of an institution which allowed sexual degradation of black women and forced an acceptance of the double standard for white women. As Harriet Jacobs writes of her perversely vindictive mistress Mrs. Flint, ". . . I, whom she detested so bitterly, had far more pity for her than [her husband] had, whose duty it was to make her life happy." When the subject matter of the narratives changed during and after Reconstruction, de-emphasizing the horror of slavery and concentrating instead on the contributions of blacks, freedwomen such as Kate Drumgoold in 1898 and Annie Burton in 1909 wrote of their former mistresses with affection and emphasized female nurturance in the slave-mistress relationship. . . .

In each of these two autobiographies the white women's sexual jealousy becomes perverse cruelty, and the black women are victimized again and again by their mistresses' displaced rage at their husbands' lechery. In describing these white women as enraged monsters, these two early women writers seem to view their mistresses as specters of slavery itself. Far from adhering to the code of the Cult of True Womanhood, which demanded piety and morality, the white women become evil creatures, nurtured by the institution which allows them and their husbands absolute power over other human beings. It is as if white women perceive the slave woman's stereotypical association with sexuality to mock her mistress's socially imposed purity. Therefore Keckley's and Jacobs's autobiographies portray the white southern woman as defiled not only by her husband's sexual misdeeds but by her own acts of cruelty to the black woman.

JACOBS'S MRS. FLINT

Jacobs's Mrs. Flint is particularly cruel and Jacobs's depiction of her evil mistress deeply ironic. Yet this demonic portrait is drawn against a background of the slave girl's early happiness with a mistress who taught her to read and write and who was "so kind . . . that I was always glad to do her bidding." Actually, though, even this kind mistress fails her because, at the white woman's death when Jacobs is twelve, the slave girl is bequeathed to the five-year-old daughter of her former mistress's sister, the ogress Mrs. Flint. Jacobs had hoped to be freed by her kind mistress and feels the provisions of her will a direct personal betrayal. She writes bitterly:

> My mistess had taught me the precepts of God's Word: "Thou shalt love thy neighbor as thyself." "Whatsoever ye would that men should do unto you, do ye even so unto them." But I was her slave, and I suppose she did not recognize me as her neighbor. I would give much to blot out from my memory that one great wrong. As a child, I loved my mistress; and, looking back on the happy days I spent with her, I try to think with less bitterness of this act of injustice.

This same "kind" mistress also reneged on a promise to young Linda's grandmother that, upon her death, the old slave woman should be freed. Instead, when the estate is settled, Dr. Flint, the old mistress's brother-in-law, dispatches "Aunt Marthy" to the auction block where, luckily, a family member buys her for fifty dollars and sets her free.

It is small wonder that Jacobs has a difficult time forgiving her former mistress's "one great wrong." From the time she is sent to the Flints, her young life becomes a nightmare punctuated by Dr. Flint's lechery and his wife's jealousy. To maintain some control over her life, young Linda, then fifteen, takes a white lover and has two children whom Mrs. Flint immediately assumes are her husband's own offspring. When the Flints decide to "break in" her children on the plantation, Jacobs, realizing that they are being punished because of her, runs away, hides in the home of a sympathetic white woman, and then is concealed in a casketlike space of a shed attached to the roof of her grandmother's house through which she bores a peephole in order to watch her children as they play. After seven years of this living death, Jacobs manages to escape to Philadelphia—a physical and emotional wreck.

Motivated as she was to write her narrative by abolitionist supporters and by her own outrage, Jacobs is scathingly ironic in her discourse, particularly as it applies to Mrs. Flint. In the actions of her mistress toward her and toward other black women, Jacobs sees not only the cruelty perpetrated by the system but also the hypocrisy of the slavocracy. Jacobs has a strong sense of the moral responsibilities of women in an immoral society, and her vivid depictions of Mrs. Flint's immorality are designed to shock those who believed that the plantation mistress was, as Catherine Clinton puts it, "the conscience of the slave South." She describes Mrs. Flint as "totally deficient in energy" but with "nerves so strong, that she could sit in her easy chair and see a woman whipped, till the blood trickled from every stroke of the lash." The white woman's Christianity is a sham: with biting irony Jacobs writes that Mrs. Flint

> was a member of the church; but partaking of the Lord's supper did not seem to put her in a Christian frame of mind. If dinner was not served at the exact time on that particular Sunday, she would station herself in the kitchen, and wait till it was dished, and then spit in all the kettles and pans that had been used for cooking. She did this to prevent the cook and her children from eking out their meagre fare with the remains of the gravy and other scrapings.

Mrs. Flint's sins are cataloged in horrendous detail throughout *Incidents*. Like Prue's fictional mistress in *Uncle Tom's Cabin,* she locks the cook away from a nursing baby for a whole day and night. Jacobs relates an incident in which her mistress makes her walk barefoot on a long errand through the snow. Later in the narrative, Jacobs gives an account of Mrs. Flint's treatment of her aunt, who, although she had many miscarriages, is forced to lie at her mistress's door each night to listen for the white woman's needs. When Aunt Nancy dies, a victim of mistreatment all of her life, Jacobs writes with the deepest irony, "Mrs. Flint took to her bed, quite overcome by the shock." The mistress "now [becomes] very sentimental" and demands that the body of the black woman whose health she has wrecked "by years of incessant, unrequited toil, and broken rest" be buried "at her feet" in the white family plot. Though dissuaded from that wish by a minister who reminds her that the black family might wish to have some say in the matter, "the tender-hearted Mrs. Flint" makes a pretty picture at Aunt Nancy's funeral "with handkerchief at her eyes."

MRS. FLINT'S JEALOUSY

Mrs. Flint's most memorable characteristic, though, is the jealous rage which she directs toward young Harriet, the hapless victim of Dr. Flint's lust. Her mistress's behavior bears brutal testimony to Jacobs's plaint: "I would rather drudge out my life on a cotton plantation, till the grave opened to give me rest, than to live with an unprincipled master and a jealous mistress." Jacobs paints Mrs. Flint's jealousy as a kind of madness brought on by the institution of slavery and sees herself, the beleaguered slave girl, and the scorned white woman as its mutual victims. She feels a kinship for her mistress: "I never wronged her, or wished to wrong her; and one word of kindness from her would have brought me to her feet." Yet that kinship is not reciprocated. Like many southern white women whose husbands were guilty of philandering with slave women, Mrs. Flint is totally blind to the plight of the female slave. "She pitied herself as a martyr," writes Jacobs, "but she was incapable of feeling for the condition of shame and misery in which her unfortunate, helpless slave was placed." Mrs. Flint "would gladly have had me flogged . . . but the doctor never allowed anyone to whip me."

When Jacobs's first child is conceived, Mrs. Flint, thinking it is her husband's offspring, vows to kill the young woman. The jealous Dr. Flint, whose injunction against violence does not extend to his own, throws Harriet down a flight of stairs, shears her hair, and beats her. In her account of Mrs. Flint, Jacobs stresses also the woman's desire to dominate. When she is sent away to the plantation of Dr. Flint's son and has worked there for five years, Jacobs must wait on the

Jealous of the sexual relationships between female slaves and their masters, white mistresses often savagely abused the slave women who served them.

table at which the visiting Mrs. Flint is served. "Nothing could please her better than to see me humbled and trampled upon," the black woman writes. "I was just where she would have me—in the power of a hard, unprincipled master. She did not speak to me when she took her seat at table; but her satisfied, triumphant smile, when I handed her plate, was more eloquent than words." When Jacobs runs away, the enraged Mrs. Flint is reported to have said, "The good-for-nothing hussy! When she is caught, she shall stay in jail, in irons, for one six months, and then be sold to a sugar plantation. I shall see her broke in yet." Throughout Jacobs's account, Mrs. Flint is depicted as struggling for control of young Harriet, and later of her children. The white woman equates these blacks to animals to be conquered and tamed. As Jacobs depicts her, Mrs. Flint is at the same time horribly vindictive and pitifully weak. She longs to control her husband's sexual appetites, but cannot. Instead she transfers her rage to Jacobs and her children and attempts, also unsuccessfully, to control them as symbols of the lust which her husband embodies.

Jacobs writes so bitterly and so thoroughly about Mrs. Flint that she seems at times to transform *Incidents* into a vehicle of rage directed toward her former mistress. If the slave narrative is indeed a means of controlling past experiences and asserting personal order upon social indignity, then *Incidents* is surely the artifact created by Jacobs's impulse to control and dominate, in language, those who controlled and dominated her. She imbues her descriptions of Mrs. Flint with terrible irony and bitterness. In so doing, she, as narrator, dominates and manipulates Mrs. Flint. She herself becomes the old slave woman with a dead, cruel mistress about whom she relates an anecdote. When the mistress dies, Jacobs writes, the old slave woman who has borne the brunt of her many beatings and cruelties steals into the room where the dead woman lies. "She gazed a while on her, then raised her hand and dealt two blows on her face, saying, as she did so, 'The devil is got you now!'" Like the old slave, Jacobs flogs her powerless former mistress over and over throughout her narrative. At long last the slave woman controls the plantation mistress, and the vehicle of that domination, language, becomes infinitely more powerful and more resonant than the lash or the chain could ever be.

KECKLEY'S JEALOUS MISTRESS

Unlike Jacobs, Keckley dispenses with her years of bondage in the early part of her autobiography. Yet her focus, like Jacobs's, centers on the brutality of a southern mistress with "a cold jealous heart." Keckley is more reticent than Jacobs about her master's sexual coercion, which resulted in the birth of her only child. But it is easy to read between the lines. Like Jacobs, young Keckley was sent to a new master and mistress when she was in early puberty. When she was eighteen and had grown into "strong, healthy womanhood," her master Mr. Burwell, a Presbyterian minister, and his "helpless" ill-tempered wife moved from Virginia to Hillsboro, North Carolina, taking Keckley, their only slave, with them.

It is at this point that Keckley's tortures begin. Her mistress, Keckley writes, "seemed to be desirous to wreak vengeance on me for something," and "Mr. Bingham, a hard, cruel man, the village schoolmaster" became Mrs. Burwell's "ready tool." At her mistress's behest, Keckley undergoes a series of savage beatings and personal exposure at the hands of the sadistic schoolmaster. In addition, Keckley suffers violent abuse in the Burwell home—in which she has a chair broken over her head. When even the perversely cruel Bingham refuses to whip the black woman again, Mrs. Burwell urges her husband to "punish" her. Mr. Burwell, Keckley writes with grim irony, "who preached the love of Heaven, who glorified the precepts and examples of Christ, who expounded the Holy Scriptures Sabbath after Sabbath from the pulpit," cuts the heavy handle from an oak broom and beats her so brutally that her bloodied condition, she writes, touched even the "cold, jealous heart" of her mistress. (Mrs. Burwell's "pity" more likely was motivated by the probability of losing a valuable piece of property, her only maid.)

Up to this point in Keckley's narrative the Burwells' sadism appears motiveless. Keckley writes only that the beatings were to "subdue [her] pride." But their motives, particularly Mrs. Burwell's, crystallize as the black woman admits that the savage actions of owners "were not the only things that brought me suffering and deep mortification." In her half-apologetic account of her own sexual coercion Keckley chooses her words carefully. Her hesitant, tentative story shows above all a continuing psychological enslavement to the white man and to a cardinal rule that the black woman must never reveal the name of the father of her mulatto child. It also paints the minister Burwell as even more of a perverse monster. Not only does he force sex upon the slave woman; he beats her savagely even after his cruel wife begs him to desist. Burwell is a prime example of [civil rights activist Angela] Davis's and [literary critic Bell] Hooks's theory that sexual domination of female slaves was an avenue to power for the white male and that rape became in the slave South a symbol of white man's total dominance over blacks and over women. Burwell dominates Keckley through sex and through violence; and although the hesitancy in her account of sexual coercion may be partly ascribed to nineteenth-century reticence on such topics, it is also testimony to a prevailing fear of the immense power of the southern white man:

> I was regarded as fair-looking for one of my race, and for four years a white man—I spare the world his name—had base designs upon me. I do not care to dwell upon this subject for it is one that is fraught with pain. Suffice it to say, that he persecuted me for four years, and I—I—became a mother. The child of which he was the father was the only child that I ever brought into the world. If my poor boy ever suffered any humilating pangs on account of birth, he could not blame his mother, for God knows that she did not wish to give him life; he must blame the edicts of that society which deemed it no crime to undermine the virtue of girls in my then position.

> Among the old letters preserved by my mother I find the following, written by myself while at Hillsboro'. In this connection I desire to state that Robert Burwell is now living at Charlotte, North Carolina.

In this account and in the letter which follows it, Keckley mentions "griefs and misfortunes" which result in family disapproval. From her specific mention of Burwell, we can infer that he was the father of her child, Keckley's account of Burwell's sexual aberrations restores, by contrast, a more sympathetic view of her mistress. It is she who finally falls on her knees and begs her husband to stop beating Keckley. Faint glimmerings of a sympathetic portrait emerge from this part of the narrative. In her former mistress Keckley shows us a white woman warped by her husband's perverse will to sexually dominate a female slave. Her sadism is horribly engendered by his lust for power.

We wonder how representative Mrs. Flint and Mrs. Burwell are. An unpublished study of the role of plantation mistresses in the lives of slaves shows mistresses to have been responsible for only a small portion of punishments inflicted upon slaves. Yet the study, in which Elizabeth Craven surveyed nineteenth- and twentieth-century slave narratives, also shows that many incidents involving the cruelty of a mistress also concerned a female slave's alleged intimacy with the master. Clinton, who cites the study in *The Planta-tion Mistress,* summarizes Craven's findings: "When [male] slaveowners sexually harassed or exploited female slaves, mistresses sometimes directed their anger, not at their un-faithful husbands, but toward the helpless slaves." In writing about the white women who transferred their jealous rages to them, Jacobs and Keckley evoke the autobiographical process as an avenue toward understanding and order. It is only through confrontation with the human evil of slavery that the freedwoman can reorder experience, redefine her place in the world, and assert her human rights. Keckley and Jacobs see their relationships with their former mistresses as paradigmatic of the essential evil of slavery—the perver-sity of that "peculiar institution" which transformed victim into victimizer and severed potential bonds of sisterhood. By recreating Mrs. Flint and Mrs. Burwell and their "cold, jeal-ous heart[s]," these two black women writers rise in lan-guage from the ashes of their enslavement and create them-selves anew—as ontological selves, as nonvictims.

The Portrayal of Slave Women in Slave Narratives

Hazel V. Carby

Hazel V. Carby, the author of *Reconstructing Woman-hood: The Emergence of the Afro-American Woman Novelist*, suggests that male slave narrators and female slave narrators portrayed woman differently. Male narrators generally portrayed slave women as victims of beatings and sexual abuse. This treatment of their mothers, wives, sisters, and daughters resulted in the emasculation of the male slaves, because they could not protect the women under their care. Female slave narrators, however, depict women not as passive victims but as activists resisting oppression. In resisting the brutality of slavery, slave women challenged the convictions of true womanhood of the mid-nineteenth century. To make her case, Carby uses narratives authored by Lucy Delany, Kate Drumgoold, and Mary Prince.

An analysis of slave narratives by men reveals a conventional portrayal of mothers, sisters, and daughters as victims, of either brutal beatings or sexual abuse. The victim appeared not just in her own right as a figure of oppression but was linked to a threat to, or denial of, the manhood of the male slave. Black manhood, in other words, could not be achieved or maintained because of the inability of the slave to protect the black woman in the same manner that convention dictated the inviolability of the body of the white woman. The slave woman, as victim, became defined in terms of a physical exploitation resulting from the lack of the assets of white womanhood: no masculine protector or home and family, the locus of the flowering of white womanhood.

The issue of miscegenation, in male slave narratives, provided a narrative occasion for the juxtaposition of the figure of the mistress with that of her female slave. A double victimization was often constructed usually in the form of a mother, sister, or daughter who became subject to the sexual abuse of the master and subsequent physical and mental abuse by the mistress. A classic instance of this type of juxtaposition occurred in the history of Ellen Craft, as told by her husband, William Craft, in *Running a Thousand Miles for Freedom* (1860). Ellen's father was her first master, her mother his slave. Ellen was almost white in color,

> so nearly so that the tyrannical old lady to whom she first belonged became so annoyed at finding her frequently mistaken for a child of the family, that she gave her when eleven years of age to a daughter, as a wedding present. This separated my wife from her mother, and also from several other dear friends. But the incessant cruelty of her old mistress made the change of owners, or treatment so desirable, that she did not grumble much at this cruel separation.

The slave man's desire for action to prevent abuse to mother, daughter, sister, or wife, or to take revenge against their brutal treatment, had in William Craft's words, "to be buried beneath the iron heel of despotism."

WOMEN SLAVES AS ACTIVE AGENTS

In contrast, in the slave narratives written by black women the authors placed in the foreground their active roles as historical agents as opposed to passive subjects; represented as acting their own visions, they are seen to take decisions over their own lives. They document their sufferings and brutal treatment but in a context that is also the story of resistance to that brutality. Lucy Delany, in *From the Darkness Cometh the Light, or Struggles for Freedom,* related her mother's fight for her own and her children's freedom after their father was sold down South. Lucy's mother had been born in a free state and kidnapped into slavery. Having successfully planned and encouraged the escape of her eldest daughter, Nancy, to Canada, Lucy's mother subsequently rebelled against the authority of her mistress and was taken to the auction block and sold to the highest bidder. Three weeks later she escaped to Chicago but was tracked down under the fugitive slave law. Fearing the revenge that could be taken against Lucy, her mother decided to return with her captors. Undaunted, however, she eventually sued successfully for her own freedom on the grounds that she was originally kidnapped. In her mother's absence Lucy's trial began. Her spirit of independence, engendered by her mother, led her to argue with her mistress, who threatened her with a whipping. Lucy rebelled against such a beating, and arrangements were made for her to be sold. Lucy's mother fought a long court case to sue for the freedom of her daughter, pleading that as a free woman she could not have given birth to a slave, and won her case.

The narrative of Lucy Delany used conventions of heroism and greatness, normally associated only with the adventurous group of male slave narratives. Her mother's virtues, declared Lucy, were as "bright rays as ever emanated from the lives of the great ones of the earth," though to others, Lucy added, she would appear to have only "the common place virtues of an honest woman." Such comments worked on two levels to disrupt conventional patterns of expected female behavior. In the absence of a male to protect and preserve the family, Lucy elevated her mother's actions to the realm of heroism, transferring codes of conventional male sexuality. But Lucy's second statement carried an understated irony, for the "common place virtues" were those denied to the black woman within the dominant ideology of womanhood. Gaining recognition as an "honest woman" was the struggle of Lucy's mother throughout the text.

Lucy and her mother were represented as a mutually supportive unit; they worked together and survived. Kate Drumgoold's narrative, *A Slave Girl's Story* (1895), also included an account of a female family unit working to support each other when the mother had finally gathered them all together after separation. These female households were portrayed as complete families, even if not conventional in structure. The authors did not describe such family structures as aberrant because they lacked a male head of household. Mothers were constructed as figures to be emulated by their daughters writing the narratives. Drumgoold described her mother's defiance of the term *slave* in phrases similar to the praise Delany reserved for her mother. "My mother was one that the master could not do anything to make her feel like a slave and she would battle with them to the last that she would not recognize them as her lord and master and she was right."

In the narrative by Mary Prince, *A West Indian Slave* (1831), such a female household was entirely absent. Mary

Prince was sold away from her mother, and each of her sisters was sold to a different master. Mary did receive teaching in rudimentary spelling from Fanny Williams, the daughter of Captain and Mrs. Williams, to whom she was sold and, later in her life, stressed that both she and the daughter of a later master were beaten. In this way Prince established in her narrative that certain sympathies and similarities could exist between a white woman and her black female slave. However, *A West Indian Slave* also revealed a conscious perception of the consequences of Prince's black womanhood in its essential difference from white womanhood. Prince demonstrated her awareness of the attempt to reduce her to nonwoman, to nonhuman, in the description of her sale. She was valued as a breeder. She was handled and examined like cattle, Prince stated, while prospective buyers "talked about my shape and size in like words . . . as if I could no more understand their meaning than the dumb beasts." Through her narrative, Prince was able to affirm her ability to judge those who would deny her humanity and to morally condemn those masters who threatened her sexual autonomy.

QUESTIONING THE CONVENTIONS OF TRUE WOMANHOOD

While the portrayal of black women as defiant, refusing to be brutalized by slavery, countered their representation as victims, it also militated against the requirements of the convention of true womanhood. As Caroline Gilman, a white, Southern, antebellum "lady" wrote in her *Recollections of a Southern Matron*: "the three golden threads with which domestic happiness is woven . . . [are] to repress a harsh answer, to confess a fault, and to stop (right or wrong) in the midst of self-defense, in gentle submission." The attempt to establish an independent and public narrative voice meant that black women had to counter simultaneously the implications of their exclusion from being women, as defined by the cult of true womanhood, and their representation as victim, whether of rape or of barter.

Frances Foster, in *Witnessing Slavery*, has documented the conventional pressures that shaped the slave narrative to conform to the demands of the reading public. Foster argues that in order to sell and to function as part of the movement for the abolition of slavery, "the viability of the slave family had to be denied, to increase the pathos of the homeless victim." As a consequence of this, Foster continued, the rare instances of nuclear family relationships in slave narratives were highly romanticized. Marion Starling, in her work on slave narratives, has emphasized the importance of conventional uses of adventure, especially in relation to escape. However, both Foster and Starling concentrate mainly on male slave narratives. Neither critic feels that an alternative mode of analysis is necessary for examining female slave narratives. From the few examples of slave narratives by women given so far, it can be seen clearly that the viability of the slave family was not necessarily denied in those narratives published after abolition but could even be asserted as effective without the presence of male heads of households. Slave narratives by women, about women, could also mobilize the narrative forms of adventure and heroism normally constituted within ideologies of male sexuality. However, these portraits of black women did not eliminate association with illicit sexuality, nor did they contradict conventional interpretations of black female sexuality. Rather, the cult of true womanhood drew its ideological boundaries to exclude another definition of black women from "woman." The image of the strong, nonsubmissive black female head of a household did not become a positive image, but, on the contrary, because it transgressed what Gilman referred to as the three "golden threads," it became a figure of oppressive proportions with unnatural attributes of masculine power. Independent black women were destined to become labeled black matriarchs.

[Nineteen-sixties activist] Angela Davis, considering slavery as a source of stereotypes of black women, has pointed to the links between the image of the matriarch and accusations of complicity between black women and white men in the subordination of the black man. Sexual relations between black women and white men are often used as evidence of the existence of such complicity during the existence of the slave system. Thus, the institutionalized rape of black women has never been as powerful a symbol of black oppression as the spectacle of lynching. Rape has always involved patriarchal notions of women being, at best, not entirely unwilling accomplices, if not outwardly inviting a sexual attack. The links between black women and illicit sexuality consolidated during the antebellum years had powerful ideological consequences for the next hundred and fifty years. . . .

Though the cult of true womanhood did not remain the

dominant ideological code, it should be remembered that the exclusion of black women from dominant codes of morality continued throughout the century. In 1895, the catalyst for the formation of the National Association of Colored Women was a public attack on the immorality of all black women. In Harriet Jacobs's slave narrative, . . . a coherent framework for a discourse of black womanhood emerged for the first time. However, the rape of black women in the South continued to be an institutionalized weapon of oppression after emancipation, and the representation of the struggle for sexual autonomy was to remain a crucial organizing device of the narrative structures of black women writers.

CHAPTER 5

The Slave Narrative's Enduring Legacy

Slave
Narratives

Harriet Beecher Stowe's Use of Slave Narratives

Robert B. Stepto

Robert B. Stepto is the author of *From Behind the Veil: A Study of Afro-American Narrative* and other critical studies of African American literature. In this essay, Stepto discusses Harriet Beecher Stowe's use of slave narratives in her composition of *Uncle Tom's Cabin,* her great antislavery novel that appeared in book form in 1852. Stepto points out that Stowe corresponded with Frederick Douglass during the writing of *Uncle Tom's Cabin,* and she modeled her African American characters, Uncle Tom and George Harris, after the protagonists of Douglass's, Josiah Henson's, and Henry Bibb's slave narratives. In modeling her characters after the protagonists of slave narratives, Stowe created "a kind of bifurcated, black antislavery hero."

In July 1851, a scant month after the Washington, D.C., *National Era* had begun its serialization of *Uncle Tom's Cabin,* Harriet Beecher Stowe wrote Frederick Douglass a rather spirited letter. She began politely with a request for Douglass's assistance in acquiring accurate information about the details of life and work on a southern cotton plantation, but soon thereafter shifted her subject and tone, taking Douglass to task for what she understood to be his critical view of the church and of African colonization. Both parts of this letter tell us something about the composition of *Uncle Tom's Cabin* and are suggestive as well about what may be termed the countercomposition of [Douglass's] "The Heroic Slave."

Stowe's request of Douglass is expressed in this way:

> You may perhaps have noticed in your editorial readings a series of articles that I am furnishing for the Era under the title of "Uncle Tom's Cabin or Life among the lowly"—In the course

Excerpted from Robert B. Stepto, "Sharing the Thunder: The Literary Exchanges of Harriet Beecher Stowe, Henry Bibb, and Frederick Douglass," in *New Essays on Uncle Tom's Cabin,* edited by Eric J. Sunquist. Copyright © 1986 Cambridge University Press. Reprinted with permission from Cambridge University Press.

of my story, the scene will fall upon a cotton plantation—I am very desirous to gain information from one who has been an actual labourer on one—&. it occurs to me that in the circle of your acquaintance there might be one who would be able to communicate to me some such information as I desire—I have before me an able paper written by a southern planter in which the details &. modus operandi are given from *his* point of sight—I am anxious to have some more from another standpoint —I wish to be able to make a picture that shall be graphic &. true to nature in its details—Such a person as *Henry Bibb*, if in this country might give me just the kind of information I desire you may possibly know of some other person—I will subjoin to this letter a list of questions which in that case, you will do me a favor by enclosing to the individual—with a request that he will at earliest convenience answer them.

Above and beyond what I sense to be a remarkable admixture of civility and imperiousness, two features of this statement warrant mention. One is that, although Stowe was undeniably an armchair sociologist of the South, here she appears to be rather assiduous in gathering southern testimony and in seeking the forms of black testimony that could both counter and corroborate the white testimony she already had in hand. The idea of weighing white and black testimony alike in order to gain a "picture" of plantation life that is "true to nature" was probably anathema to most white southerners of the late 1850s. But Stowe's practice here shows clearly that, contrary to the opinion of many southern whites . . . , she did assay southern views, white and black, while composing *Uncle Tom's Cabin.*

The other signal feature is Stowe's reference to Henry Bibb. Bibb was a Kentucky slave, born probably in 1815, who escaped from bondage only to return repeatedly to Kentucky to rescue his family as well. None of his efforts met with success; indeed, at one point, Bibb was recaptured and sold "down river" with his family to slaveholders in the Red River region. Further attempts to escape as a family were also thwarted. Eventually, Bibb once again escaped on his own, arriving in Detroit, but only after additional trials of bondage, including a time in which he was the property of an Indian slaveholder, and after another brave effort to save Malinda, his wife, which ended when he discovered she had become her master's favorite concubine. Bibb's account of his story was published in 1849 under the title *Narrative of the Life and Adventures of Henry Bibb, An American Slave, Written By Himself;* it was undoubtedly one of the principal slave narratives discussed in antislavery circles during the period in which *Uncle Tom's Cabin* was being composed and first serialized.

HENRY BIBB'S NARRATIVE

Interest in Bibb's narrative continues today. . . . Among its enduring features is Bibb's story of his Indian captivity, an account that places the narrative in the popular tradition of captivity narratives and that, however obliquely, touches upon a key issue of Bibb's day—whether the practice of slaveholding should be allowed to expand into the Indian Territories, especially once they had become states of the Union. Another key feature is Bibb's love for and dedication to his still enslaved family, particularly as repeatedly expressed in his willingness to venture back across the Ohio River, deep into the bowels of danger, in order to attempt their rescue and release. His portrait of family unity against the odds (unity up to a point—since, as we know, Bibb was eventually compelled to abandon them) unquestionably struck a chord with the abolitionists of the 1850s, who brought it forth as further proof of slavery's sinful assault upon the slave's effort to maintain a semblance of Christian home life. Moreover, it is one of the accounts that has encouraged historians of our time, including Herbert Gutman and John Blassingame, to insist that the slave family could and did, in Gutman's words, "develop and sustain meaningful domestic and kin arrangements."

A third feature, as central to Bibb's narrative as the portrait of family life, is his caustic view of the complicity between the church and the institution of slaveholding. Although Bibb is presented by his guarantors—abolitionists in Detroit—possibly out of necessity as a member of a Sabbath school and a man of "Christian course," it is clear in the body of *his* text that he has been variously wounded by the conduct of American Christians, and that as a result he is suspicious of them and "their" church. Fairly early in the *Narrative,* for example, Bibb makes his way back south in quest of his family, but is captured by a mob of slaveholders and soon imprisoned in Louisville. Of the mob, he says:

> In searching my pockets, they found my certificate from the Methodist E. Church . . . testifying to my worthiness as a member of that church. And what made the matter look more disgraceful to me, many of this mob were members of the M. E. Church, and they were the persons who took away my church ticket, and then robbed me also of fourteen dollars in

cash, a silver watch for which I paid ten dollars, a pocket knife for which I paid seventy-five cents, and a Bible for which I paid sixty-two and one half cents. All this they tyranically robbed me of, and yet my owner, Wm. Gatewood, was a regular member of the same church to which I belonged.

Much later in the narrative, after Bibb and his family have been sold into an abominable state of bondage in Louisiana, he records the following about his new master, a church deacon:

And while I was offering up my prayers to that God who never forsakes those in the hour of danger who trust in him, I thought of Deacon Whitfield; I thought of his profession, and doubted his piety. I thought of his handcuffs, of his whips, of his chains, of his stocks, of his thumb-screws, of his slave driver and overseer, and of his religion; I also thought of his opposition to prayer meetings, and of his five hundred lashes promised me for attending a prayer meeting. I thought of God, I thought of the devil, I thought of hell; and I thought of heaven, and wondered whether I should ever see the Deacon there. And I calculated that if heaven was made up of such Deacons, or such persons, it could not be filled with love to all mankind . . . as we know it is from the truth of the Bible.

In light of these pronouncements, grounded as they were in the most bitter of experiences, it is not surprising that Bibb claims elsewhere in his story that "I never had religion enough to keep me from running away from slavery in my life."

Finally, Bibb's *Narrative* endures as much for its figurative language as for its rhetoric and ideology. I refer here to Bibb's descriptions of the Ohio River (which separated freedom in Ohio from bondage in Kentucky) as a road to freedom and, for the bonded black, a river Jordan. The most remarkable passage in this vein begins:

Sometimes standing on the Ohio River bluff, looking over on a free State, and as far north as my eyes could see, I have eagerly gazed upon the blue sky of the free North, which at times constrained me to cry out from the depths of my soul, Oh! Canada, sweet land of rest—Oh! when shall I get there? . . .

STOWE'S RELIANCE ON BIBB'S NARRATIVE

I have quoted at some length from Bibb's narrative principally to suggest that Mrs. Stowe's interest in it may not have been limited to Bibb's account of life on Red River cotton plantations (for which, see his chapters X–XII). At the very least, I would argue that her portrayal of Eliza Harris's escape to freedom across the ice patches of the Ohio River was prompted in part by Bibb's high symbolism of the Ohio as a pathway of freedom. It also seems clear that Bibb's allegiance to his family gave impetus to Stowe's portraits of the Harris family and of Tom's family as well. It also seems altogether possible that Stowe's George Harris is a fictive Bibb—in his light skin, which would have abetted his escape, and in his vociferous allegiance to family, his vivid dreams of freedom in Canada, and his occasional grave doubts about the social and moral efficacy of Christian practice.

In short, Stowe's story of George and Eliza Harris is roughly that of Henry and Malinda Bibb, once a happy outcome to the Bibbs's plight has been, as some nineteenth-

THE ADVENTURES OF HUCKLEBERRY FINN AND THE SLAVE NARRATIVE

Critic Lucinda Mackethan claims that the slave narrative was a source for Mark Twain as he penned his most famous novel, The Adventures of Huckleberry Finn.

The movement from escape to freedom and the concept of escape as freedom give form and content to Huck's story, and this design for *The Adventures of Huckleberry Finn* has provided the shape for many subsequent quests for freedom that we find in American literature. Hemingway was most probably thinking of Huck's gift for idiomatic language when he asserted that "All modern American literature came from one book by Mark Twain called Huckleberry Finn. . . . It's the best book we've had . . . there was nothing before. . . ." It would be easy to conclude that there was also "nothing before" for Mark Twain to use as a model for Huck's indelible brand of lighting out. However, the very words *escape* and *freedom* uttered in connection with American idealism call up what would seem an almost unavoidable source of stimulation. As a writer from a slave state whose book explores the drama of conscience and whose character Jim is an articulate fugitive slave, Mark Twain would have many reasons to consult the narratives of slaves who had successfully made the escape that was finally beyond Jim's power to complete. The question of influence remains largely speculative, but we can certainly establish the point that a consideration of parallels between the American fugitive slave narratives and *The Adventures of Huckleberry Finn* enlivens and deepens our understanding of both.

Lucinda H. Mackethan, "Huck Finn and the Slave Narratives: Lighting Out as Design," *Southern Review* 20.2 (1984), pp. 247–64.

century pundits liked to say, "bestowed." Altogether, Stowe's debt to Bibb's *Narrative* is as great as that she incurred while reading another 1849 narrative, *The Life of Josiah Henson, Formerly a Slave, Now an Inhabitant Of Canada, as Narrated By Himself.* Much has been made over the decades, some by Stowe herself, of Tom's resemblance to Henson, and of how Henson's escape to Canada may have inspired Stowe's presentation of the Harrises' settlement there. But when we study the texts alone, it is clear that the parallels between George Harris and Bibb are as pronounced and that Bibb's experiences on a Red River cotton plantation probably had as much to do with the composition of *Uncle Tom's Cabin* as did Henson's escape to Canada. Indeed, Harris in Canada is something of a Henson and a Bibb, much as Tom in Louisiana is both a Bibb and a Henson.

CREATING A BLACK ANTISLAVERY HERO

If Stowe's novel favors Henson's text, the evidence is in her treatment of the two subjects that take up the balance of her 1851 letter to Douglass. Having made her request of him and referring to Bibb in the process, Stowe writes:

> —I have noticed with regret, your sentiments on two subjects,—the church—&. African Colonization—&. with the more regret, because I think you have a considerable share of reason for your feelings on both these subjects—but I would willingly if I could modify your views on both points.

Nothing comes of her intention to debate Douglass's criticisms of African colonization. But in what remains of the letter, she is thoroughly impassioned in defending the church: She is, as she says, a minister's daughter, a minister's wife, the sister of six ministers, and she thereby chooses to take questions of the church's stand on slavery as in some measure charges against her own and her family's conduct. Having defended herself and her kin ("it has been the influence that we found *in the church* & by the altar that has made us do all this"), Stowe ends her letter in this way:

> After all my brother, the strength &. hope of your oppressed race does lie in the *church*—In hearts united to Him . . . Every thing is against you—but *Jesus Christ* is for you—&. He has not forgotten his church misguided &. erring though it be. . . . This movement must &. will become a purely religious one. . . . christians north &. south will give up all connection with [slavery] &. later up their testimony against it—&. thus the work will be done.

Given these views, it is not surprising that in *Uncle Tom's Cabin* Stowe created both Tom and George Harris, and chose to present them, albeit in rough, nearly unrealized fashion, as a kind of bifurcated, black antislavery hero—one almost white, the other very black; one hot-tempered, the other stoic to the point of meekness; one impelled by circumstances farther and farther north, the other farther and farther south; one central to her narrative ideologically, as an emblem of African colonization, the other central spiritually, and hence the "better half" of Stowe's hero, since he is emblematic of exalted Christian faith. The curiosity of this construction is that, although Tom is the "better" and true hero of Stowe's novel, whose character and presence create strong ties between her own and Henson's text—ties that would endure well into the remainder of the century through the other publishing activities of Stowe and Henson alike—it is in George Harris, not Tom, that Stowe confronts what were for her and other white Americans the most troubling issues in the antislavery debate, and confronts as well the tone and argument of the more problematic (though doubtless inspiring) slave narratives of the late 1840s: those of Bibb, Douglass, and a few other miscegenated hotheads. In Tom, Stowe expresses her consuming respect for Henson. In George Harris, she creates a composite portrait of Bibb, Douglass, and the rest of their type; and although she honors them throughout the bulk of her long novel, judiciously imagining how they, had they been Harris, would have responded to a given crisis or turn of events, she also sends them packing, first to Canada and then to Liberia. In short, the paragraphs on African colonization missing from Stowe's letter to Douglass are to be found in the chapters of *Uncle Tom's Cabin* that she would write soon after. She revises the close of Bibb's *Narrative,* where it is evident that he resides not in Canada but (still) in the United States, and replies as well to Douglass's many criticisms of the church and colonization alike, suggesting that he might just consider, in light of his views, removing not merely from Boston to Rochester, as he had just done, but from the Afro-American's New World to his Old.

The Slave Narrative and the Early African American Novel

Marva J. Furman

The slave narrative had a profound effect on the development of the African American novel. In this essay, Marva J. Furman of the University of Michigan-Flint discusses the slave narrative's influence on the first African American novels, such as *Clotel; or, The President's Daughter* by William Wells Brown, *Iola Leroy; or, Shadows Uplifted* by Frances E.W. Harper, and *Blake; or, The Huts of America* by Martin Delaney. According to Furman, these early African American novels rely on the slave narrative for their structure, plot conventions, and subject matter. Furman provides evidence that the first African American novelists read the slavery narratives of the mid-nineteenth century and learned of the stories of slaves in the abolitionist press. The slave narratives, as Furman contends, "engender the aesthetic of the early Afro-American novel and in many instances lay the groundwork for the novelists' treatment of fictional, imaginative content."

Partly because of the narrative's overwhelming historical significance in piecing together the realities of slave life, but primarily because of its contemporary political influence, not enough interest has been shown in its literary value. Such critics as Vernon Loggins have denied that it has any literary value. The assumption is that the dual roles—that of writer as advocate and that of writer as artist—are irreconcilable. In the words of Allen Tate, the black writer has been limited "to a provincial mediocrity in which feelings about one's difficulties become more important than [literature] itself." Fortunately, however, not all critics agree with Tate's

Excerpted from Marva J. Furman, "The Slave Narrative: Prototype of the Early Afro-American Novel," in *The Art of Slave Narrative: Original Essays in Criticism and Theory*, edited by John Sekora and Darwin T. Turner. Copyright © 1982 Western Illinois University. Reprinted with permission from Marva J. Furman.

assessment. Other critics assert that the black literary aesthetic must be distinguished from a "white" aesthetic. In the philosophy articulated by the late Franz Fanon, critical tools for evaluation must be determined by the cultural experiences which give meaning to the art. Similarly, in his analysis of a writer's role, Addison Gayle points out that,

> Not autotelic, the novel, like its sister genres, depends upon the creative genius of the author, which, heightened by political, social, and historical factors, depicts the experiences of man and, reaching beyond form and structure, communicates with men everywhere. The novel is the one genre which attempts in dramatic and narrative form to answer the questions, what are we? and what is it all about.

These critics, of course, are speaking of fiction, and my purpose is not to suggest that slave narratives be evaluated as works of fiction. I do suggest, however, that in addition to its socio-historical value, the narrative may also have a literary significance. For once we accept the black novelist's dual role—that of advocate and that of artist—then we may also recognize that his commitment to social change did not begin with publication of the first black novel, but has its genesis in the narrative. More specifically the black aesthetic espoused by the early novelists, those writing between 1853 and 1900, developed in response to the anti-slavery activities which permeated the nineteenth century, foremost among which was the narrative. Any comprehensive discussion of the novel, then, must necessarily include a discussion of the narrative, and it may be seen that in many ways the narrative is a predecessor and analogue to the early novel. Certainly the only literary genre of the period that espoused an aesthetic similar to that of the novel was the slave narrative; both were instruments of protest. For example, in outlining his purpose for writing *Clotel; or, The President's Daughter,* William Wells Brown, the first black American novelist, wrote:

> If the incidents set forth in the following pages should add anything new to the information already given to the public through similar publications, and should thereby aid in bringing British influence to bear upon American slavery, the main object for which this work was written will have been accomplished.

Forty years later, in a note at the end of her novel *Iola Leroy; or, Shadows Uplifted* (1893), Frances E.W. Harper establishes criteria for evaluation of her work:

> From the threads of fact and fiction I have woven a story whose mission will not be in vain if it awakens in the hearts of our countrymen a stronger sense of justice and a more Christlike humanity in behalf of those whom the fortunes of war threw homeless, ignorant, and poor upon the threshold of a new era.

These criteria are quite similar to those established many years earlier by narrators like Henry Bibb, who was motivated by a desire to shed light and truth "on the sin and evils of slavery as far as possible," or like J.W.C. Pennington, who sent "forth the third edition of *The Fugitive Blacksmith* as an humble harbinger to prepare and keep the way open; that the world may be acquainted with the question and that everyone may be well aware of the unreasonable claims urged by the planters and utter impossibility of their maintaining them." In general, then, there is no sharp distinction of literary aesthetic between the novel and the narrative of this period.

THE STRUCTURE OF SLAVE NARRATIVES

A closer analysis of the narrative reveals other influences upon the novel. The basic stages of development of these slave narratives are discussion, itemization, and dramatization. Typically, the narrator becomes the protagonist whose mission is to combat an evil world. Thus, the horrible details of the slave's life in general are discussed, followed by dramatizations of the cruelty inflicted upon the narrator. Also dramatized is the narrator's educational growth and moment of realization when he opens his eyes to the possibility of escape. This episodic structure based on the hero's mistreatment, education, escape, and consequent abolitionist work strongly influenced the structure of novels like Martin Delaney's *Blake; or, The Huts of America* and James Howard's *Bond and Free*. It would also seem that many of the plot devices found in the novels are drawn directly from the narratives. A good illustration is Delaney's *Blake*. The location of the plotted slave revolt in the South as well as the Red River region of Louisiana, which Delaney used as the locale for his examination of plantation conditions, is used in much the same way in the narratives of Northup and Bibb. Similarly, the escape stratagem used by Bibb during his flight from slavery is identical to that used by Delaney's protagonist, Henry Blake. Each escapes from the plantation by carrying a bridle enabling him to claim he is searching for his master's horse.

The novelist is indebted to the narrator not only for his episodic structure and certain plot conventions, but also for certain adaptations of subject matter as well. For example, Brown's attacks upon Southern Christianity and Southern white preachers in *Clotel* directly parallel Pennington's and others' condemnation of slavery because of its responsibility for sins of the slave. Other themes that run through many of the novels come from the narratives: the theme of the tragic mulatto, the theme of miscegenation, and the concern with the ironic contrast between the colonists' fighting for their freedom while denying it to blacks. The concrete diction, ironic humor, understatement, polemics, melodrama, characterizations, points of view, subject matter, and structure that we recognize in the early black novel all appear first in the narrative.

These similarities are not just coincidental. While there is no record of the novelists' having publicly acknowledged the narratives' literary influence on their art, there is evidence which suggests that the novelists read these personal histories. Indeed, the first blacks to write fiction were employed by the anti-slavery agency, and were thoroughly familiar with vehicles of propaganda—the oral and written slave narratives. In fact, the pre–Civil War fiction may be seen as the maturation of an oral/literary genre which began on the lecture platform where ex-slaves dramatized aspects of their early lives and of the cruel dehumanization which was inflicted on them while enslaved. With the founding of several abolitionist publications and the development of the American Anti-Slavery Society in New England, the written narrative achieved fruition and importance in the fight for freedom. Thus, from 1813 onward, we see a narrative style characterized by the use of irony to attack the fundamental inconsistency of having slavery in a Christian and democratic nation. As more lecturers gained experience on the platform and in print, the narratives became more standardized and more dramatic. The move from dramatized history to historical fiction was not long in coming.

ART NURTURED ON ABOLITIONIST LITERATURE

Of the nine authors who published fiction before 1900, the first three published before 1865, and all three nurtured their art on anti-slavery literature of the period. In his discussion of the American Anti-Slavery Society, Vernon Loggins suggests the pervasive quality of abolitionist propaganda. He points out that at its first convention, held in 1833, the Society,

> called for the engagement of agents to be sent far and wide for the purpose of lecturing, scattering tracts and pamphlets, receiving subscriptions for the antislavery newspapers, and spreading abolition propaganda in every way possible. The psychological effect upon the public of the Negro as an anti-slavery agent was soon recognized. By 1838, Charles Lenox Remond, a Massachusetts Negro, had begun his long career as an abolition agent for various New England societies. In 1839, Samuel Ringgold Ward, born a slave in Maryland, became an agent for the American Anti-Slavery Society. The number of Negroes so employed after 1840 grew in leaps and bounds.

By 1830 more than fifty black anti-slavery societies had been founded, and several anti-slavery publications had been initiated. By 1819 Charles Osborn had founded two abolitionist newspapers, *The Philanthropist* in Ohio and *The Manumission Intelligencer* in Tennessee. In 1821 Benjamin Lundy founded *The Genius of Universal Emancipation* in Ohio. In 1827 the first black newspaper, *Freedman's Journal,* began publication in New York City. In 1831, the most famous of the abolitionist newspapers, William Lloyd Garrison's *Liberator,* was founded in Boston.

Another famous paper, Frederick Douglass's *The North Star,* began publishing in New York on December 3, 1847, and is a fine example of the reading fare to which the novelists were treated. In addition to selections from widely read English and American authors, original lyrics, book reviews and general-information articles on the literary scene and the English language, Douglass printed selections from slavery-inspired literature. Such titles as the following appeared: "Helen Wilson; or The Quadroon's Triumph—A Tale of the Times" [anonymous] (October 5, 1855); "The Creole Slave Betrayed" from *Our World; or, The Slaveholder's Daughter* (October 12, 1855); "The Heroic Slave Woman" by Reverend Samuel J. May (February 4, 1853); "Black Chloe" by Fanny Fern (August 6, 1854); and "Poor Nina, The Fugitive" from *Ups and Downs* by Cousin Cicely (January 5–12, 1855). In addition to these stories written by those who had claimed to witness the atrocities of which they wrote, Douglass published slave narratives, which as a genre had inspired the eyewitness accounts. One of the most popular narratives was

Douglass's own story, *My Bondage and My Freedom* (August 1855 through December 1855). Another popular narrative, Northup's *Twelve Years a Slave* (1853), was advertised, reviewed, and quoted in the newspaper. Thus, in printing these anti-slavery pieces *The North Star* was important as an arbiter of cultural and literary taste for its 4,500 subscribers, many of whom were black. Indeed, blacks supported abolitionist publications in large numbers. J. Noel Heermance, in discussing the *Liberator*, points out that,

> only two months after the launching of Garrison's *Liberator* in 1831, Philadelphia Negroes under William Whipper, Robert Purvis, and James Forten supported and contributed to its maintenance. In fact, in the earliest and most trying years of the *Liberator*, the number of Negro subscribers far outweighed the number of white supporters, so that in 1831, 400 of that newspaper's 450 subscribers were Negro; and, even as late as 1834, seventy-five per cent of its more than 2,300 subscribers were Negro.

Clearly, then, concerned blacks consumed liberal doses of abolitionist literature. The pre–Civil War novelists were no exception; they, too, heard the lectures and read the slave-inspired narratives and stories.

MARTIN DELANEY'S *BLAKE*

Delaney is one example of a novelist thoroughly familiar with abolitionist literature. He was born free in 1812 in Charlestown, Virginia, where he lived until moving with his parents to Chambersburg, Pennsylvania, at the age of ten. They later settled in Pittsburgh, where Delaney grew up. His career as an activist and literary figure is interesting and quite varied. He studied medicine at Harvard Medical School, initiated a scheme for colonizing blacks in Central America, achieved the rank of major in the United States Army after the Civil War, and became a national political figure. In 1843 he began publication of a black newspaper in Pittsburgh, the *Mystery*, and issued it regularly until 1847 when he helped Douglass found *The North Star*. His association with the *Star* lasted until 1851. And perhaps the triumph of his literary career, *Blake; or, The Huts of America*, was serialized and published in *The Anglo-African Magazine* from January through July, 1859 (it was not until 1970 that all but the final chapters were found in the files of *The Anglo-African*).

It is generally agreed that Delaney began writing *Blake*

around 1853, the publication date of Northup's narrative. These parallel dates may account in part for Delaney's use of the same Louisiana locale of which Northup writes. Delaney's knowledge of slave narrative material is made clear in his attack upon *Uncle Tom's Cabin,* which appeared in 1852, one year before he began *Blake.* Delaney condemned *Uncle Tom's Cabin* because Mrs. Stowe "knows nothing about us," and had found the main value of the book to be its use of slave narrative materials. Delaney, too, used slave narrative materials, but unlike Mrs. Stowe's, his main theme is black insurrection, and his protagonist is based on the heroic rebel figure of Nat Turner.

The works of other pre–Civil War novelists were also strongly influenced by abolitionist literature. Frank G. Webb's *The Garies and Their Friends* (1857) is concerned to a large extent with abolitionist themes. Harper's *Iola Leroy* was not published until 1892, but the author's art was developed during the abolitionist struggle. Thus, as early as 1854 she published verse in which slavery is the dominant theme: "The Slave Mother," "The Slave Auction," "The Fugitive's Wife," and others.

CLOTEL AND THE CRAFTS' NARRATIVE

The most impressive example of the extent to which slave literature influenced the development of a work of fiction is Brown's *Clotel* (1853). It is probably no accident that the first novelist and playwright was also an ex-slave, who told his story many times from the lecture platform before putting it in print in 1847. The move from slave narrative to abolitionist novel was inevitable. In the novel Brown uses the same ironic tone, the abolitionist themes, and some sketches from his own narrative. But more importantly, he incorporates sketches from another famous narrative, William and Ellen Craft's *Running a Thousand Miles for Freedom.* The Crafts' narrative was not published until 1860, seven years after Brown's *Clotel,* but Brown had heard the story of the Crafts' daring escape many years before, when he shared the lecture platform with the couple, and each worked for the Anti-Slavery Society. In the year following their escape from Georgia to Pennsylvania, Brown introduced the Crafts to the first evening session of the seventeenth annual meeting of the Massachusetts Anti-Slavery Society, which was held in Fanueil Hall (Boston) on January 24, 1849. During the next four months the three lectured throughout Massachusetts until May, when Brown left to attend the annual meeting of the American Anti-Slavery Society in New York.

The Crafts' lectures, like their narrative, began with minor details of their lives, followed by many anecdotes illustrating the plight of the female slave, and concluded with a recital of their exciting escape. In *Clotel* Brown incorporates two of the more sensational aspects of the Crafts' narrative. Just as Ellen's aunt was married to her master, and at his death sold as a slave, one of Brown's main characters meets with the same fate. And just as William and Ellen escape with Ellen disguising herself as a white man and William masquerading as her slave, so Clotel escapes from Virginia in disguise with another slave passing as her black servant. *Clotel*, then, is typical of the pre–Civil War fiction influenced by the narrative.

Of the five or six fiction writers who published between 1865 and 1900, most had their social consciousness shaped by reconstruction and post-reconstruction periods. Their writings speak of disfranchisement, segregation, and white violence. Yet most exhibit the urgency of the abolitionist novel, and many retain the same themes. Charles Chesnutt, J. McHenry Jones, Frances E.W. Harper, and Pauline Hopkins, for example, still wrote ironically of America as a Christian and democratic country, and of the tragic mulatto. The influence of the narrative is far reaching.

The narratives, then, must not be viewed simply as autobiographies with historical significance. For while one must recognize that the content of the narratives is not fictional, one could also conclude that certain of those narratives published between 1820 and 1860 do engender the aesthetic of the early Afro-American novel and in many instances lay the groundwork for the novelists' treatment of fictional, imaginative content.

The Slave Narrative and Twentieth-Century African American Autobiography

Lucinda H. Mackethan

The slave narrative made a lasting impact on African American writing; most profound has been its impact on twentieth-century African American autobiography. Richard Wright, Malcolm X, and other African American authors of autobiographies have used the structure and form of the slave narrative to tell their life stories. This essay, by Lucinda H. Mackethan of North Carolina State University focuses on Wright's *Black Boy*, his story of growing up in the segregated South and escaping to a more racially tolerant environment. According to Mackethan, Wright's autobiography, published in 1945, "bears indelibly the stamp of the slave narrative in its shape and strategies of voicing; it is widely acclaimed as the culmination of the slave narrative heritage in modern times." Mackethan connects *Black Boy* to slave narratives authored by Frederick Douglass and William Wells Brown.

In 1845, Frederick Douglass, who had escaped from slavery to become a powerful speaker for the abolition movement, published a detailed narrative of his life from childhood to manhood as a slave. In part he was motivated in this endeavor by charges that a man of his eloquence and erudition could not possibly have come from such an oppressive environment as the slavery world he depicted in his speeches. Thus a "written life" was shaped to validate a "lived life," as Douglass and other fugitive slaves who published narratives of their lives in the years of frantic pro- and anti-slavery sen-

Excerpted from Lucinda H. Mackethan, "Black Boy and Ex-Coloured Man: Version and Inversion of the Slave Narrator's Quest for Voice," *CLA Journal*, vol. 32, pp. 123–47, December 1988. Reprinted with permission from the College Language Association.

timent before the Civil War returned through voice and memory to the scenes of their suffering, re-creating their experience of bondage and freedom over and over again.

One hundred years after Douglass published the first of his three autobiographies, Richard Wright published *Black Boy*, subtitled *A Record of Childhood and Youth.* The similarities between his story of his boyhood in the South and Douglass' *Narrative of the Life of Frederick Douglass, An American Slave: Written by Himself* have often been noted. In terms of themes they record a boy's struggle against violence and ignorance, his growth into awareness of his needs and rights as a human being in a world denying that status, and his formulation of a plan to educate himself and to flee his oppressors. In terms of narrative arrangement, both autobiographies give detailed treatment to scenes of cruelty, rebellion, and education, while the actual flight to freedom and the writer's attainment of the status which defines his place at the time of telling are hardly inferred at all by narrated event. The voice that tells each of these tales itself becomes, during the very process of recollecting the past, the agent of the drama of the protagonist's future achievement of manhood and freedom.

Certainly Wright used the model of the slave narratives in shaping his version of quest for a voice with which to announce and confirm his struggle for freedom. The slave who escaped bondage and wrote a first-person account of his enslavement was demonstrating his new position not just of freedom but of mastery with every word he wrote. When Frederick Douglass paused in his account of hearing slaves sing to say, "I did not, when a slave, understand the deep meaning of those rude and apparently incoherent songs. I was myself within the circle; so that I neither saw nor heard as those without might see and hear," he was confirming himself as the maker of meaning, freeing himself from the circle that held him in ignorance, and authenticating his position of control over not just his own life but the world that he was calling up for judgment. Richard Wright, whose story of his life very much concerns the same quest for mastery as man and artist, uses, as we shall see, a narrative strategy very similar to Douglass' in this passage. As James Olney says, *Black Boy is* "composed simultaneously of narration and commentary, past experience and present vision, and a fusion of the two in the double 'I' as Richard, the 'black boy' of fifteen, twenty, and thirty years earlier, and 'I' as 'Richard Wright,' a mature intellectual, an accomplished writer brooding over his life and its meaning.". . . .

BLACK BOY: THE VOICE OF THE SLAVE NARRATIVE

Black Boy bears indelibly the stamp of the slave narratives in its shape and strategies of voicing; it is widely acclaimed as the culmination of the slave narrative heritage in modern times. [Critic Robert] Stepto, pointing out Wright's close relationship to Frederick Douglass in matters of tone and organization, goes beyond other critics in also assessing some essential differences: the "voice" assumed by Wright's persona "is very much in the Afro-American heroic grain" of Douglass; however, Stepto says, Wright "does not want to suggest (as Douglass does) that the achievement of voice may yield even a fleeting sense of personal ease and of community, for that would disruptively suggest that his persona has found a measure of comfort and stability in the very world he is about to leave." Wright, then, uses in *Black Boy* many of the same kinds of scenes that the slave narrators utilized to demonstrate their struggle for a freedom synonymous with manhood and fulfilled selfhood. Still, his alienation from his environment is more penetrating, a more pervasive factor in the makeup of his personality. Here a comparison of naming scenes is instructive. William Wells Brown tells us in his slave narrative how he kept his original name of "William" as a means of defying his master's will and indicating the inviolability of his inborn identity, yet for his surname he added "Wells Brown" to honor his first white benefactor and, we might conjecture, to symbolize a new identity based on human rather than racial kinships. Richard Wright, when it came to naming himself as the subject of his autobiography, chose the name and title "Black Boy" to indicate the irony of his position and the persistence of racial stereotypes denying a human community of names. Writing of this choice of a title to his publishers, he said, "It is honest. Straight. And many people say it to themselves when they see a Negro and wonder how he lives. Black Boy seems to me to be not only a title but also a kind of heading of the whole general theme." Title, name, being, and theme are thus the coverage around Wright's central concerns—that the Negro will always be a "boy" to the white world, which disallows his manhood because he is black; that boyhood and blackness are states of mind to be overcome through ironic voicing, and that freedom and manhood must be struggled for and won through an "honest, straight" confrontation of cultural absolutes with individual human realities.

The title of Wright's autobiography indicates that he will stress the totality of the oppression he faces, often over the potentiality of the self-image he is shaping. This does not mean that he will not be recording his ultimate mastery of the world which he must experience; it actually means that he is more exclusively dependent on voice than on the slave narrators for his verification of himself. There are no abolitionists, no Wells Browns, in Wright's autobiography. There is only, always alone, a speaker who in the first chapter shows himself, at age four, hiding from his parents in terrible fear and who in the last chapter shows himself hiding his feelings from his white coworkers. As he is about to leave for the North, one of these whites tells him, "You'll change. Niggers change when they go north"; the narrator remembers thinking, "I wanted to tell him that I was going north precisely to change, but I did not. 'I'll be the same,' I said, trying to indicate that I had no imagination whatever." Here *Black Boy* testifies to its speaker-protagonist's mastery of his own imagination as a means of fulfilling himself through voice. His mastery is shown in three contexts—first as both threatened and paradoxically nurtured by violence; secondly as denied both by black familial and white cultural environments; thirdly as confirmed through the individualized, expressive use of language to convey images of growth and fulfillment.

For the black boy, imagination offers the magic power to lift an imposed circle away from the imprisoned self simply through the exercise of perception. The display of such a power, as Wright knew when he was talking to his white coworkers, was a declaration of freedom that the South—white culture generally—could not acknowledge and still hope to keep the black boy in his place. The violence inherent in the act of imagination is illustrated in *Black Boy's* first chapter, in which Richard, because he is bored and lonely, sets fire to the living room curtains. As a result, not only does the house burn, but also Richard is beaten almost to death by his mother. Wright, ordering his life into art, opens his self-presentation with an event which illustrates, first, that his protagonist wants to use but cannot control his imagination and, second, that he is learning to associate imagination with rebellion and violent punishment, but also with attention. Shortly after this scene is another that links imagination with violence but also with something much more useful, language. When Richard's father is annoyed at

Richard Wright

the sound a kitten makes and tells his son to "kill that damn thing," Richard is aware that there are levels or, in Douglass' words, "degrees," of meaning involved in the command. Richard's insistence on a literal meaning which he knows his father does not intend is, in this case, an act of imagination designed to aid rebellion, through manipulation of language, with violent consequences.

When Richard asks the questions that would explain the true contexts of the words he hears and the things he sees, his attempts to learn are met with the same response that Frederick Douglass had noted one hundred years earlier—a violent verbal rebuff or even a harsh slap. Richard's own weaknesses are the only things that the world, including his family, seems to want to him to discover. Yet all the attempts to restrain his curiosity cause the opposite effect, stimulating the growth of an imagination that finally takes Richard beyond the circles formed around him. This effect is similar to that noted by slave narrator [James] Pennington, who recalled that he ceased to think of himself as a slave only after he had been provoked into thought by a severe beating by his master. Fear of whites becomes, for Richard, the most powerful stimulant of all to the onset of active imagining: "My spontaneous fantasies lived in my mind because I felt completely helpless in the face of this threat [White violence] that might come upon me at any time. . . . My fantasies were a moral bulwark that enabled me to feel that I was keeping my emotional integrity whole."

LYING TO SURVIVE

To link "fantasies" and "integrity" as Wright does might seem illogical, but with what he called his "predilection for what was real" and his world's preference for deception, Wright understandably was led to count on what he could create in his own mind for truth. Richard is taught by whites and blacks alike that the acceptable means of gaining advantage is to lie. Yet he cannot comply: "I would remember and dissemble for short periods, then I would forget and act straight and human again." Three instances of lying reveal how closely the speaker-protagonist in *Black Boy* connects his freedom to honor his imagination's integrity with his ability to survive on his own terms in a hostile world. When he tries to explain to his grandmother what he has done in writing his first story ("It's just a story I made up," he pleads), her reply shows her world's distrust of mind: "Then it's a lie," she snaps.

A second incident of lying dramatizes the inversion of standards in a society based on race prejudice. When Richard graduates from high school, he is asked to be valedictorian and writes his speech, only to be informed that he is expected to read something his principal has written. When he refuses, the principal says, "Wake up boy. Learn the world you're living in." Yet Richard insists, "I know only a hell of a little, but my speech is going to reflect that." Having found a voice, he had found himself, and he is not willing to deny either. In a scene which echoes William Wells Brown's practicing his name on the road that leads North, Richard and a friend practice their graduation speeches: "Day in and day out we spoke to the trees, to the creeks, frightening the birds, making the cows in the pastures stare at us in fear." For the growing Richard, who he is can be contained in every word he speaks; if he lies, he cancels his identity, and if he establishes his own voice, he has the power to make the world "stare in fear."

A final instance of lying is perhaps the most symbolic one in revealing how the protagonist learns at last to master and direct an imagination nurtured in violence and threatened by the encircling world's demand for distortion. In Memphis, Richard reads in a newspaper a denunciation of H.L. Mencken; like Frederick Douglass when he heard the white Southerners denouncing "abolition," Wright knows that he has come upon a name that will mean something helpful to him. Wanting to read some of Mencken's works, Richard schemes for a way to get books from the all-white "Public" library and finally finds a white man who will loan his card. To check books out, Richard must "forge a note" to the librarian and sign the white man's name. Richard's consenting to forgery, to a written lie, a lie involving the taking of a false identity, is explicable when we see the creativity involved in his act. To forge might mean to deceive, but it also means to create, as James Joyce dramatized when he had Stephen Dedalus [of *A Portrait of the Artist as a Young Man*] talk of "forging" in the "smithy" of his soul "the uncreated conscience" of his race. Forging becomes a name for the process of the creative shaping of life that the narrative voice in *Black Boy* confirms through his "made up" work, ordered to present a self freed from the distorting, limited vision imposed upon it by its culture.

FLEEING NORTH

That Richard Wright finally reached his destination of freedom is a matter not disclosed in the narrative through detailing of event. Our last clear image of him is "in full flight aboard a northward bound train"; yet, like Douglass', his arrival in the North is confirmed most effectively by the voice which throughout has been evaluating as well as presenting the story of a young man's evolution into a narrator whose tale presupposes the freedom and, by extension, the manhood and selfhood of the teller. The voicing of the tale for Wright and the slave narrators is both a predicted last act for their dramas and an ever-present reminder of who the teller is and the distance he has covered in his journey to his present place.

The function which Richard Wright shaped for his double voice was essentially the same as the slave narrators', yet through his handling of it he also gave expression to new problems of freedom and identity facing the modern black writer. Ralph Ellison, addressing Wright's achievement in *Black Boy,* wrote in a 1945 review that his autobiography "has converted the American Negro impulse toward self-annihilation and 'going-under-ground' into a will to confront the world, to evaluate his experience honestly and throw his findings unashamedly into the guilty conscience of America." It is significant to note that Ellison also began work in the summer of 1945 on a novel in which a first-person, autobiographically inclined, "underground" voice narrates a naive protagonist's struggles to transcend his own ignorance and to free himself from a white culture's imprisonment. Ralph Ellison's Invisible Man exhibits patterns of experience that make him similar, in some ways, to Richard Wright's Richard.

Toni Morrison's Use of the Slave Narrative in *Beloved*

Joycelyn K. Moody

The fictional slave narratives of the later half of the twentieth century are evidence of the slave narrative's enduring legacy. Toni Morrison, winner of the Nobel Prize in Literature, is an example of a novelist of the late-twentieth century who uses the form and plot of the slave narrative in her fiction. This essay, published by Joycelyn K. Moody while she served as Scholar-in-Residence at Kalamazoo College, focuses on Morrison's use of the slave novel in her 1987 novel *Beloved*. According to Moody, *Beloved* has much in common with Harriet Jacobs's *Incidents in the Life of a Slave Girl*. Nonetheless, the texts differ in the treatment of literacy, community, and romantic love. For Jacobs, literacy is the tool that leads to freedom and selfhood. Morrison's protagonist Sethe, however, is illiterate; literacy is used by her white masters as a tool of oppression. She must gain self-esteem through romantic love and a connection to her community.

Perhaps the most poignant and best known antebellum slave narrative of a black American woman is Harriet Jacobs's *Incidents in the Life of a Slave Girl: Written by Herself* (1861). Published 125 years later, two neo-slave narratives—*Beloved* (1987), by Toni Morrison, and *Dessa Rose* (1986), by Sherley Anne Williams—also chronicle the experiences of slave women. These contemporary novels have much in common with Jacobs's nineteenth-century autobiography. Each is, at its core, the story of a slave mother's concerns for herself and her children as she attempts to escape to freedom. In addition, each details physical abuse suffered by slaves in general, sexual and psychological abuse of slave women in par-

Excerpted from Joycelyn K. Moody, "Ripping Away the Veil of Slavery: Literacy, Communal Love, and Self-Esteem in Three Women's Slave Narratives," *African American Review*, vol. 24, Winter 1990. Reprinted with permission from *African American Review* and the author.

ticular; each frequently "interrupts" its linear narrative with flashbacks, sermons, songs, or other commentary; and each develops, though to significantly different degrees, the major themes of literacy, community, and self-esteem.

However, one important phenomenon distinguishes Jacobs's text from Morrison's and Williams's: Jacobs's narrator writes her story, but the two fictive slave women cannot. At the outset of their narratives, they are illiterate. . . .

What I hope to do in this essay is to consider the treatment of the common themes of literacy, community, and romantic love in relation to the self-esteem of the central characters *of Incidents, Beloved,* and *Dessa Rose* [not discussed in this excerpt]. Literacy dominates the themes of Jacobs's text, not coincidentally perhaps, because she writes in an era in which literacy is the exception to the rule among black women. In her work, notably, romantic love is least developed; the only discussion of it appears in chapter 7, "The Lover." On the other hand, the modern texts imply a kind of paradox; they are highly rhetorical texts that seem to devalue rhetoric. In them, literacy seems less significant than communal or conjugal love in the lives of women who must *tell* rather than *write* their stories as a means of crystallizing their escape to freedom. Garnering sufficient self-esteem to relate their pasts depends on the active support of an attentive audience. I believe the contemporary writers' emphases on communal love, which includes romantic love, and the responsibilities of community evolve from their uniquely modern preoccupation with such antitheses of community as estrangement and isolation. So, finally, I want to speculate here on how the neo-slave narratives differ from their antebellum literary counterparts.

JACOBS'S EMPHASIS ON THE POWER OF LITERACY

Jacobs's *Incidents in the Life of a Slave Girl* privileges literacy and community over romantic love as it describes the self-actualization of its narrator, a woman who names herself Linda Brent. Jacobs's rhetorical text illustrates her belief, with other antebellum autobiographers, that "knowledge is power, and the fundamental source of knowledge is literacy, the ability . . . to liberate other minds with a text of one's own." Also, like most *female* antebellum slave autobiographers, Jacobs writes out of a need to recognize and to represent the collective experiences of the community of blacks and white women who aided her. Primarily, of course, Jacobs writes to assert herself and to document her personal experiences as a slave girl. . . .

By the time she writes *Incidents,* Jacobs's faith in language is well-placed, for letters to Norcom (or "Flint") that she adroitly composed in captivity have prevented her capture. Nonetheless, Jacobs seems caught in part in the cult of true womanhood, and faces a moral dilemma. Through Brent, she calls for a revised moral code for slave women, insisting, ". . . I feel that the slave woman ought not to be judged by the same standards as others," yet twenty pages later she laments, ". . . I was no longer worthy of being respected by the good and pure." Throughout the text, the narrator moves back and forth between public debate and private confession, between the political and the personal. Similarly, she shifts from one verb tense to another, particularly when begging forgiveness for her sexual "misuse" of "Mr. Sands," the man who fathered her children. Indeed, it is often difficult to tell whether Brent has forgiven *herself* for seducing one white man to repel the advances of another. For instance, she writes on one page, "I will not try to screen myself behind the plea of compulsion from a master; for it was not so. Neither can I plead ignorance or thoughtlessness. . . . I knew what I did, and I did it with deliberate calculation." Then on the following page, she writes, "I know I did wrong. No one can feel it more sensibly than I do. The painful and humiliating memory will haunt me to my dying day." This "tense" shift, from past to present to future, is indicative of Jacobs's mastery over language as she at once confesses to her "virtuous readers" and seeks to manipulate them into a sympathetic community who will not condemn her. What is less clear is the extent to which Jacobs contrives the urgency in her descriptions of sexual taboos, of which she feels both victim and perpetrator.

Brent's narrative ends without ever depicting her in a satisfying romantic relationship. Very early in the narrative, she discloses her love for a free-born black carpenter, whose identity she does not divulge. When Dr. Flint refuses to allow the carpenter to buy and marry the fifteen-year-old Brent, she insists that, for her, ". . . the lamp of hope had gone out. The dream of my girlhood was over." Indeed, this is the only mention of romance in Brent's life. Instead, for love and affirmation, she relies on the Southern community that enables her to escape. After escaping, however, Brent seems more self-reliant than dependent upon community. The last chapters of *Incidents* depict various members of the narrator's Northern community, especially her two children, with whom she is reunited in New York: the employers whom she accompanies to Liverpool, where she slept, "for the first time, with the delightful consciousness of pure, unadulterated freedom"; and the white woman who eventually frees her. Though she extols her relatives and friends, she has no excessive attachment to anyone. Even as Jacobs attempts to create community within her text, communal love, like motherlove, is valued but not romanticized. Similarly, the conspicuous absence of suitors from her text suggests that Jacobs considered the possibilities of conjugal love for the black American slave woman infrequent, perhaps even injurious.

SETHE'S ILLITERACY

Unlike Brent, who "voices" Jacobs's story over 200 pages, Sethe Suggs in *Beloved* initially speaks only when necessary, avoids "rememorying" her past, which "had been like her present—intolerable," and disdains the future—all because the "one set of plans she had made . . . went awry so completely she never dared life by making more." Not until a fellow slave, Paul D, brings her past to her, along with an "easy and upfront" love, does Sethe feel safe enough to dare confront that past: "Her story was bearable because it was his as well—to tell, to refine and tell again." Upon his arrival, Sethe begins the process of reclaiming her lost self. When Sethe returns with Paul D from "her first social outing in eighteen years," she finds her daughter Beloved returned from death as a young woman, who, like Paul D, is "a catalyst for revelations as well as self-revelations." Through her, too, Sethe attempts to embrace and heal herself by recollecting her past in a series of flashbacks.

Like the slave girl Brent, Sethe loses her parents as a young girl and becomes dependent on a community of other slaves and white women. Brent, however, is much more fortunate than Sethe in three important ways: (1) She knows and admires both of her parents before their deaths; (2) her subsequent supportive community is led by a blood relative; and (3) her white mistress teaches her to read and write. Sethe, on the other hand, never knows her father, and though she sees her mother "but a few times out in the fields" before

Ma'am is hung, she remembers her distinctly. Furthermore, Sethe's community is not composed of blood kin, but only of two maimed women and a handful of slave men. Their white owners, the Garners, are kind, but do not empower their slaves with literacy.

There are other significant differences besides. While Sethe grows up chaste and, at age 15, marries the man of her choice, Brent at 15 is tormented by Flint, denied her free black lover, and within a year engages in sexual relations with Sands. Sethe's children are by her slave husband; Brent's, by Sands out of wedlock. At 21, nine months pregnant, Sethe is gang-raped, then beaten while fleeing slavery; at 21, Brent escapes to a dark and airless garret for seven years to avoid sexual abuse by Flint.

In Ohio, Sethe considers killing her children as her only means of saving them from slavery, whereas Brent's freed children live for a time as servants in New York. Sethe cuts the throat of her "crawling-already" baby girl: Brent sends her daughter to school.

The crucial differences in Brent's and Sethe's experiences arise from the ways each woman adjusts to the peculiar circumstances of her life and sexuality. As the authors of the two texts present these circumstances, the characters' adjustments center on literacy, community, and self-assertion. To be specific, in *Incidents in the Life of a Slave Girl*, Jacobs assumes and inscribes a community of readers of her text; urged by Amy Post, a white abolitionist, to tell her story, Jacobs knows as she writes that she *will* have readers, however resisting they may be of her autobiography. More importantly, Jacobs tries to create a community of radicals out of her community of readers by offering them positive behavioral models within her text. That is, by imaging Brent confessing to women in her supportive community throughout her text—in scenes with her grandmother, daughter, and employer, for example—and by recounting their forgiveness for her "sin," Jacobs makes her text both a confession and a model for radical response to her violation of the cult of true womanhood. In other words, Jacobs uses her knowledge of language to attempt the restoration of her honor and self-esteem, established in childhood by loving parents and familial security but damaged severely in adolescence by Norcom. Her text is also, of course, an account of the wrongs suffered by collective black womanhood, and a plea for a collective response by her readership—i.e., the eradication of slavery in America.

LITERACY AS A TOOL OF OPPRESSION

Through its depiction of Sethe, who lacks Brent's ability to narrate a personal or a public story "written by herself," *Beloved* condemns the dehumanizing proclivities of literacy and community. As a child she is deprived by slavery of her parents and of the right to literacy. But nurtured in her adolescence by the blacks at Sweet Home, Sethe develops sufficient self-esteem to resist being victimized by the written words of schoolteacher, Mrs. Garner's brother-in-law, who is summoned to the plantation upon the master's death. For Morrison, schoolteacher represents "not only the Age of Enlightenment but its twin, born at the same time, the Age of Scientific Racism." When Sethe realizes why "schoolteacher'd wrap that string all over my head, 'cross my nose, around my behind. Number my teeth," she no longer thinks ". . . he was a fool." Instead, she intuits his intentions to keep her family enslaved and to promulgate his right to do so. Bearing "a big hat and spectacles and a coach box full of paper," and training his nephews to record "'her human characteristics on the left; her animal ones on the right,'" schoolteacher proposes to document the natural superiority of whites. To her horror, Sethe feels a sense of complicity, and thus treachery, in the cataloguing of her people's inferiority; she says, "'I made the ink, Paul D. He couldn't have done it if I hadn't made the ink.'"

But Morrison's neo-slave narrative, itself an "illusion that it's the characters' point of view . . . a *told* story," disempowers documentation. Schoolteacher's skill with language elucidates his baseness. When Sethe realizes that schoolteacher's literacy measures his own bestiality, not hers, she determines to cease assisting him and to preserve her "best things" from his inhumanity, at any cost. Thus, viciously raped and beaten and heavily pregnant, but strengthened by motherlove, Sethe frees her family. That is, when Sethe considers the power of the written word to destroy her family, she responds to its threat by asserting herself. Because she is illiterate, she cannot assert herself as Brent does, by producing a counter-text; she cannot wield the master's weapon against the master. Sethe reacts to the tyranny of literacy in her life simply by escaping it. Literacy's power is diminished by Sethe's ability to achieve freedom without it. In fact, literacy is significant in Sethe's life only in that, embodied in schoolteacher, it robs Sweet Home of sweetness and provokes Sethe's escape, and in that, without it, she cannot disprove schoolteacher's text. But in freedom, Sethe—like Brent, who prefaces her narrative saying, ". . . it would have been more pleasant to me to have been silent about my own history"—feels no compulsion to record her past.

COMMUNITY AND SELF-ESTEEM

Things alinguistic and preverbal—the Sweet Home slaves' assumption of Sethe's native worth, the luxury of six years of marriage to Halle Suggs, her victorious trek to Ohio, the miracle of a renegade white girl to aid her—all simply confirm Sethe's faith in her individual ability to achieve whatever goals she sets for herself, freedom included: "'I did it. I got us all out. . . . I had help, of course, lots of that, but still it was me doing it; me saying, *Go on*, and *Now*. Me having to look out. Me using my own head.'" In Ohio, she has a month of "unslaved life," twenty-eight days during which she elects to share her story with a free community:

> Days of healing, ease and real-talk. Days of company: knowing the names of forty, fifty other Negroes, their views, habits; where they had been and what done. . . . One taught her the alphabet; another a stitch. All taught her how it felt to wake up at dawn and *decide* what to do with the day.

Sethe's new-found community is, however, short-lived. For on the twenty-ninth day of her free life, after she hosts in gratitude a "feast for ninety people who ate so well, and laughed so much, it made them angry," the community turns away when schoolteacher and his nephews come to reenslave Sethe. Realizing that white men could not have made it to her home on Bluestone Road without being seen by her neighbors, and thus that she is without communal support, when schoolteacher again threatens her family's safety, Sethe collects "every bit of life she had made, all the parts of her that were precious and fine and beautiful, and carried, pushed, dragged them through the veil, out, away, over there where no one could hurt them." Terrified by the heavy scent of her neighbors' disapproval, and determined against recapture, Sethe resolves to slay her children.

In depicting the malevolence and treachery of the Cincinnati community, Morrison's narrator, like her protagonist, is bent on tearing "through the veil" that hides the effects of enslavement. Whereas Jacobs's text subscribes to the conventions of nineteenth-century polite discourse and antebellum "moral absolutism," Morrison's contemporary novel thoroughly lacks sentimentality as it details "'slavery's monstrous features.'" Though there is nothing gratuitous in the description of Sethe's slitting her daughter's throat, for example, there is nothing covert in it either. Sethe later recalls only the sting of hummingbirds' beaks in her skull, but the narrator unabashedly details what schoolteacher finds: "Little nigger-boy eyes open in sawdust; little nigger-girl eyes staring between the wet fingers that held her face so her head wouldn't fall off; little nigger-baby eyes crinkling up to cry."

Defining her duty as a novelist in 1987, Morrison stated,

> My job becomes how to rip that veil drawn over "proceedings too terrible to relate." The exercise is also critical for any person who is black, or . . . marginalized . . . for, historically, we were seldom invited to participate in the discourse even when we were its topic.

According to this definition, the contemporary (black) writer, a century after Reconstruction, is to function more like the *post*bellum slave narrator than like the antebellum slave narrator, to which he/she is more often compared. That is, postbellum slave narrators, such as Elizabeth Keckley and Booker T. Washington, envisioned their purpose as ensuring that slavery would continue to be discussed in American letters after Emancipation and as dictating "the discursive conventions in which their past would be discussed." They wrote narratives that would reassure white Americans of the humanity of their black compatriots; they emphasized former slaves' pragmatic qualities, such as physical strength, moral diligence, and material acquisition. On the other hand, Morrison's neo-slave narrative, apparently "told" by a third-person narrator as much to blacks as to whites, parallels antebellum narratives' attention to ethical social cooperation. Just as Jacobs implicitly dictates the appropriate moral response of the white women and abolitionists to whom she primarily appeals, Morrison implicitly dictates the appropriate modern response to the needs and conditions of the contemporary black American community—social reform through community service—; for led by churchwomen, Sethe's contrite neighbors acknowledge their complicity in Sethe's plight and, after eighteen years, make amends.

Even though the community in Cincinnati recognizes its moral negligence and rectifies its infraction, Sethe's equilibrium and self-esteem are not fully recovered in the course of the novel. Morrison demonstrates that the pride Sethe takes in her escape—"'it was me doing it; me saying, *Go on,* and *Now*'"—has waned to self-doubt, by echoing the self-referent at the end of the novel. When Paul D tells Sethe that she herself is her "'best thing,'" she can only reply, "'Me? Me?'" Though partly healed by the confrontations she must make in the year of the return of Paul D and Beloved, Sethe has also been nearly consumed by her estrangement from her lover and her indulgence in her ghostly daughter. Morrison posits that only through the commitment of Paul D, Sethe's second daughter Denver, and the reformed community can Sethe regain her self-esteem and integrity. Literacy seems insignificant to Sethe's process of "claiming ownership of [her] freed self," and orality, her recollections, have likewise been incidental. Only the example of Paul D's romantic love, on the one hand, and the good faith and good deeds of others like her, on the other hand, can restore Sethe to wholeness.

Conversely, the title character of *Dessa Rose* does achieve wholeness in the process of recollecting and retelling her life. However, although Toni Morrison and Sherley Anne Williams reach divergent conclusions about the relative importance of literacy and community in black Americans' lives, there are many similarities between their contemporary novels. For one, both protagonists are depicted as slave women who are initially unable to image or assert themselves in their anguish over the death of their "best thing." Also, both are first whipped, then tried at court for resisting slavery; and both eventually gain freedom and try to reconstitute themselves.

Chronology

1619

Slavery is introduced on American continent when a group of about twenty slaves kidnapped in Africa is brought to Jamestown, Virginia, and sold as plantation slaves.

1700

Samuel Sewall of Massachusetts publishes *The Selling of Joseph*, the first antislavery document published and distributed in America.

1703

The first American slave narrative, *Adam Negro's Tryall*, is recorded in the transactions of the Colonial Society of Massachusetts.

1760

The second American slave narrative, *A Narrative of the Uncommon Sufferings, and Surprizing Deliverance of Briton Hammon*, is published.

1776

The British colonies declare independence from Great Britain. The Declaration of Independence, penned by Thomas Jefferson, a Virginia slave owner, asserts that "all men are created equal; that they are endowed by their Creator with certain unalienable rights; that among these are life, liberty and the pursuit of happiness." Jefferson's antislavery comments in the draft of the Declaration are deleted before the document is issued.

1789

In England, Olaudah Equiano, a freed slave, publishes *The Interesting Narrative of the Life of Olaudah Equiano*.

1791

The free American colonies put into place the U.S. Constitution, which allows slavery.

1793

Eli Whitney invents the cotton gin, a machine that separates the cotton fiber from the seed. The machine makes cotton the king crop of the South.

1820

The Missouri Compromise outlaws slavery in United States territories north of latitude 36°30'.

1829

David Walker, a free African American living in Boston, publishes the antislavery pamphlet titled *Walker's Appeal in Four Articles.*

1831

On January 1, William Lloyd Garrison, a Massachusetts writer and orator, begins publication of the *Liberator,* an abolitionist newspaper.

The History of Mary Prince, the first slave narrative authored by a woman, is published in London. The illiterate Prince dictated her story to a white recorder.

In August, Nat Turner, a Virginia slave, leads a twelve-hour slave rebellion. Turner's Rebellion results in the deaths of sixty whites. Turner is captured on October 30, found guilty of murder, and hanged on November 11. On November 25, Thomas Gray, a lawyer who interviewed Turner before his trial, publishes *The Confessions of Nat Turner.*

1833

William Lloyd Garrison forms the American Anti-Slavery Society.

1839

After interviewing former slaves, Theodore Weld publishes *American Slavery as It Is.*

1845

Frederick Douglass, an escaped slave, publishes *Narrative of the Life of Frederick Douglass, an American Slave.*

1847

William Wells Brown publishes *Narrative of William Wells Brown, a Fugitive Slave.*

1849

Henry Bibb publishes *Narrative of the Life and Adventures of*

Henry Bibb, an American Slave.

Josiah Henson publishes *The Life of Josiah Henson, Formerly a Slave, Now an Individual of Canada.*

1850

Congress passes the Compromise of 1850, which included a strict Fugitive Slave Law.

1851

National Era, a weekly abolitionist newspaper, begins to publish a series of fictional episodes by Harriet Beecher Stowe about a fictional slave named Uncle Tom. The following year, Stowe publishes the episodes as the abolitionist novel *Uncle Tom's Cabin, or Life Among the Lowly*. The novel becomes an immediate best-seller.

1853

William Wells Brown publishes the novel *Clotel; or, the President's Daughter.*

1854

Congress passes the Kansas-Nebraska Act, which allows the citizens of those two territories to decide whether slavery will be legal when the territories become states. Proslavery and antislavery settlers clash in what becomes known as "Bleeding Kansas."

1855

Frederick Douglass publishes his second slave narrative, *My Bondage and My Freedom.*

1857

The U.S. Supreme Court issues a decision in the *Dred Scott* case. Scott, a slave, sued for his freedom after his master took him to a free territory. The Court rejects Scott's claim and asserts that the federal government could not outlaw slavery in United States territories.

1859

The abolitionist John Brown executes a raid on the federal arms arsenal at Harpers Ferry, Virginia. He intends to capture weapons, arm slaves living nearby, and begin a slave revolt. Brown is captured by U.S. Marines, tried for treason and murder, and executed.

1860

Abraham Lincoln of Illinois is elected president. Southern states begin seceding from the Union.

1861

The month after Lincoln takes office, the Civil War begins.

Harriet Jacobs publishes *Incidents in the Life of a Slave Girl*, the first slave narrative actually written by a woman.

1863

On January 1, President Lincoln issues the Emancipation Proclamation, freeing slaves in the states in rebellion against the Union.

1865

The Civil War ends.

Eight months after the end of the Civil War, the Thirteenth Amendment to the U.S. Constitution takes effect. The amendment states, "Neither slavery nor involuntary servitude, except as a punishment for crime whereof the party shall have been duly convicted, shall exist within the United States, or any place subject to their jurisdiction."

1868

Elizabeth Keckley, a seamstress living in Washington, D.C., publishes a slave narrative titled *Behind the Scenes.*

1881

Frederick Douglass publishes his third autobiography, *Life and Times of Frederick Douglass.*

1884

Mark Twain publishes his novel *Adventures of Huckleberry Finn*, the story of a white boy and a runaway slave named Jim.

1901

Booker T. Washington publishes *Up from Slavery*, the story of his rise from slavery to national prominence.

1927

A.P. Watson, a graduate student at Fisk University, interviews one hundred former slaves to record their religious conversion experiences.

1936

The Federal Writers' Project begins a two-year project to interview former slaves, resulting in the recording of the life stories of more than two thousand individuals.

1967

William Styron receives the Pulitzer Prize in fiction for his novel *The Confessions of Nat Turner.*

1976

Alex Haley publishes *Roots*, the narrative of his African ancestor, Kunta Kinte, who, in 1767 was kidnapped from his home in what is now Gambia, shipped to America, and sold into slavery. Haley's book wins a Pulitzer Prize and National Book Award.

1987

Toni Morrison receives the Pulitzer Prize in fiction for her novel *Beloved*, the story of an escaped slave woman who kills her daughter rather than allow her to be taken back into slavery.

FOR FURTHER RESEARCH

ANTHOLOGIES CONTAINING SLAVE NARRATIVES AND CRITICAL INTRODUCTIONS

William L. Andrews, ed., *From Fugitive Slave to Free Man: The Autobiographies of William Wells Brown.* New York: Penguin Books, 1993.

——, ed., *Sisters of the Spirit: Three Black Women's Autobiographies.* Bloomington: Indiana University Press, 1986.

——, ed., *Six Women's Slave Narratives.* New York: Oxford University Press, 1988.

William L. Andrews and Henry Louis Gates Jr., eds., *The Civitas Anthology of African American Slave Narratives.* Washington, DC: Civitas/Counterpoint, 1999.

John W. Blassingame, ed., *Slave Testimony: Two Centuries of Letters, Speeches, Interviews, and Autobiographies.* Baton Rouge: Louisiana State University Press, 1977.

Arna Bontemps, ed., *Great Slave Narratives.* Boston: Beacon Press, 1969.

B.A. Botkin, ed., *Lay My Burden Down: A Folk History of Slavery.* Chicago: University of Chicago Press, 1945.

Henry Louis Gates Jr., ed., *The Classic Slave Narratives.* New York: New American Library, 1987.

Henry Louis Gates Jr. and Nellie Y. McKay, eds., *The Norton Anthology of African American Literature.* New York: W.W. Norton, 1997.

Girlber Osofsky, ed., *Puttin' on Ole Massa: The Slave Narratives of Henry Bibb, William Wells Brown, and Solomon Northup.* New York: Harper and Row, 1969.

Yuval Taylor, ed., *I Was Born a Slave: An Anthology of Classic Slave Narratives.* 2 vols. Chicago: Lawrence Hill Books, 1999.

Norman Yetman, ed., *Voices from Slavery.* New York: Holt, Rinehart, and Winston, 1970.

INDIVIDUAL SLAVE NARRATIVES WITH CRITICISM AND RELATED DOCUMENTS

Frederick Douglass, *Narrative of the Life of Frederick Douglass, an American Slave, Written by Himself.* Eds. William L. Andrews and William S. McFeely. New York: W.W. Norton, 1996.

——, *Narrative of the Life of Frederick Douglass, an American Slave, Written by Himself.* Ed. David W. Blight. Boston: Bedford Books, 1993.

Olaudah Equiano, *The Interesting Life of Olaudah Equiano, Written by Himself.* Ed. Robert S. Allison. Boston: Bedford Books, 1995.

Kenneth S. Greenberg, ed., *The Confessions of Nat Turner and Related Documents.* Boston: Bedford Books, 1996.

Harriet A. Jacobs, *Incidents in the Life of a Slave Girl, Written by Herself.* Ed. Jean Fagan Yellin. Cambridge, MA: Harvard University Press, 1987.

Booker T. Washington, *Up from Slavery.* Ed. William L. Andrews. New York: W.W. Norton, 1996.

BOOKS ON THE SLAVE NARRATIVE

William L. Andrews, *To Tell a Free Story: The First Century of Afro-American Autobiography, 1760–1865.* Urbana: University of Illinois Press, 1986.

Joanne M. Braxton, *Black Women Writing Autobiography.* Philadelphia: Temple University Press, 1986.

Charles H. Davis and Henry Louis Gates Jr., eds., *The Slave's Narrative.* New York: Oxford University Press, 1985.

Paul D. Escott, *Slavery Remembered: A Record of Twentieth-Century Slave Narratives.* Chapel Hill: University of North Carolina Press, 1979.

Jennifer Fleischner, *Mastering Slavery: Memory, Family, and Identity in Women's Slave Narratives.* New York: New York University Press, 1996.

Frances Smith Foster, *Witnessing Slavery: The Development of Antebellum Slave Narratives.* Westport, CT: Greenwood Press, 1979.

———, *Written by Herself: Literary Production by African American Women, 1746–1892.* Bloomington: Indiana University Press, 1993.

Charles H. Nichols, *Many Thousand Gone: The Ex-Slaves' Account of Their Bondage and Freedom.* Bloomington: Indiana University Press, 1963.

John Sekora and Darwin T. Turner, eds., *The Art of Slave Narratives: Original Essays in Criticism and Theory.* Macomb: Western Illinois University Press, 1982.

Marion Wilson Starling, *The Slave Narrative: Its Place in American History.* Boston: G.K. Hall, 1982.

Robert B. Stepto, *From Behind the Veil: A Study of Afro-American Narrative.* Urbana: University of Illinois Press, 1979.

Kari Joy Winter, *Subjects of Slavery, Agents of Change: Women and Power in Gothic Novels and Slave Narratives, 1790–1865.* Athens: University of Georgia Press, 1992.

BOOKS ON INDIVIDUAL SLAVE AUTHORS

William L. Andrews, ed., *Critical Essays on Frederick Douglass.* Boston: G.K. Hall, 1991.

William Edward Farrison, *William Wells Brown, Author and Reformer.* Chicago: University of Chicago Press, 1969.

Eric Foner, ed., *Nat Turner.* Englewood Cliffs, NJ: Prentice-Hall, 1971.

Karen Kennerly, *The Slave Who Bought His Freedom.* New York: Dutton, 1971.

William S. McFeely, *Frederick Douglass.* New York: W.W. Norton, 1991.

BOOKS ON AMERICAN SLAVERY

John W. Blassingame, *The Slave Community: Plantation Life in the Antebellum South.* New York: Oxford University Press, 1979.

Martin Duberman, ed., *The Antislavery Vanguard.* Princeton, NJ: Princeton University Press, 1965.

William Dudley, ed., *Slavery: Opposing Viewpoints.* San Diego: Greenhaven Press, 1992.

Elizabeth Fox-Genovese, *Within the Plantation: Black and*

White Women of the Old South. Chapel Hill: University of North Carolina Press, 1988.

John Hope Franklin, *From Slavery to Freedom.* New York: Knopf, 1979.

Leslie Howard Owens, *This Species of Property: Slave Life and Culture in the Old South.* New York: Oxford University Press, 1976.

Kenneth M. Stampp, *The Peculiar Institution: Slavery in the Ante-Bellum South.* New York: Knopf, 1956.

Sterling Stuckey, *Slave Culture.* New York: Oxford University Press, 1987.

Deborah Gray White, *Ar'n't I a Woman: Female Slaves in the Plantation South.* New York: W.W. Norton, 1985.

INDEX